The
Jimmy Shand
Story

Other books from Scottish Cultural Press

The Democratic Muse: Folk Music Revival in Scotland
Ailie Munro
1 898218 10 2

Traditional Step-dancing in Scotland
JF and TM Flett
1 898218 45 5

The
Jimmy Shand
Story

Ian Cameron

Foreword by Robbie Shepherd

SCOTTISH CULTURAL PRESS
EDINBURGH

First published 1998 by
Scottish Cultural Press
Unit 14, Leith Walk Business Centre,
130 Leith Walk, Edinburgh EH6 5DT
Tel: 0131 555 5950 • Fax: 0131 555 5018
e-mail: scp@sol.co.uk
http://www.taynet.co.uk/users/scp

Reprinted March 1998

British Library Cataloguing in Publication Data
A catalogue entry for this book is available from the British Library

ISBN: 1 84017 019 0

All the photographs in this book, unless specified, have been supplied
by the Shand family or by Bill Wright of Kirkcaldy.

Printed and bound by
Cromwell Press Ltd., Trowbridge

Jimmy Shand with Ian Cameron

Foreword

The mere mention of the name of Jimmy Shand, and Scots hairts the world oer burst wi pride, proud to acknowledge the man and his music as a true symbol of their nationality. For some of us, too, there is an added pride in being accepted to share in the hame-ower family life that surrounds Windyedge at Auchtermuchty. It's a home that Jimmy would face the hazards of long night driving just to 'win hame' to his own bed and close family circle.

Thoughts, public and private then, come rapidly to mind for me and I'll open up the latter trait 'jist a thochtie' as I recall a night, some fifteen years ago, when my wife Esma was in Stracathro Hospital near Brechin having a hip operation. Jimmy had been on the telephone to me to find out which ward she was in because, as he said, 'I jist wint tae send a wee cairdie, son, fae Anne, David and masel.'

I motored down from Aberdeen on my usual evening visit and there was Esma, propped up in bed with a radiant twinkle in her eye. 'You'll never guess who I had here this afternoon! A clue – an accordion player, his wife and son.' Well, I thought of all our musician pals in the Aberdeen area but drew a blank. Yes! It was the Shands, all the way from Fife, hand-delivering the card!

I should have known better because this is typical of the man, but if further proof was needed, I got it when I went into the transport café at the end of the hospital road on my way home that evening. The lady in charge in the kitchen greeted me with: 'Ye'll never guess who was in here today, Robbie!' It was, of course, the maestro himself and he had even taken oot his box from the boot of his car to give them a tune!

As you read through the pages of this book you'll come upon many similar human stories from genuine friends who have held the Shand family in great respect over the years. It's a side that the shy smile but magic name doesn't show to the public; but why should it? It's nae what Jimmy, nor indeed Anne, who has been such a tower of strength, would ever want.

I despair of those who write even today decrying 'oor ain music', linking, in some most ignorant and patronising way, heather, haggis and Shand.

The Shand 'dunt' is unique and, from the box and its owner, has sent messages of home world wide from one of Scotland's finest-ever ambassadors.

In my role of radio presenter I have asked many a musician – Jimmy included – to put the Shand dunt into words, without too much success!

'I jist follow the feet o the best dancer on the floor, son,' was how the maestro explained his timing, but timing's just one small part of it! No matter how the band members were changed over the years round about him, the sound was still simply Shand – a canny, laid back approach belying the technical genius whose box was and is part of his soul.

Not that long ago a portrait of Jimmy was hung in the National Gallery alongside that of Niel Gow. With Jimmy's famed smile it might have been better to place him beside the Mona Lisa! That portrait and the placing of it, though, is very significant in the history of Scottish dance music. In future years I have no doubt that, with the greater awareness of our musical tradition, folk – school children, scholars, common-or-garden box players alike – will look up to the two pictures o the most influential figures on the dance scene in awe.

Both Niel and Jimmy came from a rural background, Gow arriving at a time when society dancers were creeping out of the woodwork, in the mid-1700s, having been banned by the kirk for promiscuous dancing! Niel's gliding bow and his inspired tunes became a new foundation stone – a rock that has survived the relentless waves of diverse music, pressing on our own dance scene.

So it was with Jimmy Shand in the early and mid-twentieth century, when he introduced the sound of the bothy: the humble melodeon, the forerunner of the modern accordion.

Like Gow, Jimmy too was to compose tunes to lighten the steps for the dancers' feet and provide another rock on which Scottish country dancing was to flourish.

So, music for the Society from music o the bothy. It made nae difference to Jimmy and I like to think Niel Gow had a similar approach.

Jimmy's music with the special dunt will live with me forever, as will my picture of a very happy family man that wants nae fuss.

My thoughts flow ever forward, this time to the 1995 Annual General Meeting of the National Association of Accordion and Fiddle Clubs, when musicians assemble for official business and impromptu sessions. Away from the main hall, mid-way through the afternoon, I heard a most familiar sound. Attracted to the music like a fly to a spider's web, I came on a wee ante room with a few accordionists, fiddlers, mooth-organists and the like.

Holding court was Jimmy Shand.

'Gies *Auld Robin Gray* in D, Jimmy,' – which he dutifully did.

When the wee session came to a close, I went forward to congratulate the doyen of the button-box and to say how pleased I was to see him back playing. The twinkle in the eye and the shy smile said it all.

'Robbie, man, it's the richt haun only. Sandy gaed's a caa-tee wi the left ane!'

That at the age of 87 – then as modest, but as keen on the music as ever.

It's just a pity that the powers-that-be haven't recognised fully the man who has no equal with the same enthusiasm as some of the beknighted folks who have graced the other music scenes for only a 'day and a denner'.

It's my honour to be the one chosen to guide you to these fascinating pages on a living legend.

Robbie Shepherd

Introduction

Jimmy Shand – in most countries in the world you will get some sort of reaction when people hear this name. A few unenlightened souls will bundle him in with a preconceived idea of Scotland – consisting of heather, haggis and kilts – and dismiss him without further consideration; but for many millions of others his name means a guarantee of excellence in a special blend. A gleam will come to the eye and a lump will gather in the throat. A tune will come into the head which will be hummed softly while fingers drum on the table and feet tap on the floor. Troubles will be banished for a moment as a warm remembrance of happier times comes into the mind.

I have been a Jimmy Shand fan for as long as I can remember. Still imprinted in my memory are Saturday evenings in the late forties and early fifties, tea-times at my aunt's. The routine on the radio was Sportsreel followed by the McFlannels and then – Scottish country dance music! My parents had a good collection of 78s, many of which were Jimmy Shand recordings. As the years passed, my interest in his music has grown, but it was not until 1997 that the opportunity arrived for me to meet him personally.

I am a member of Scotspeak, the oral history archive based in Fife, and was very surprised to find among their tapes some interviews with Jimmy Shand. Like many others, I had the impression he did not talk very much or give interviews, but there he was, with his long standing friend, Dr Sandy Tulloch, chatting away to Valda Hood-Chin and her husband Alistair Hood. A few months later I was introduced to Jimmy at Letham Village Hall, and the idea for this book developed.

After sounding out the possibilities with Valda, Alistair, Sandy Tulloch and Erskine Shand (Jimmy Shand Jr.), I approached Jill Dick of the Scottish Cultural Press with an outline proposal. Her response was immediate and the project quickly got underway.

The warmth of the welcome and encouragement I have received from Jimmy, his wife Anne and David, as well as Erskine and his wife Margaret, on my visits to Auchtermuchty has been greatly appreciated and I feel quite at home anytime I go.

If anyone is looking for a deep psychological analysis based on Jimmy's perceived public persona they will be disappointed as Jimmy is not a complex character. Jimmy is not even a dour man; in fact he has a wonderful sense of humour and a marvellous memory, but he is basically very shy and prefers to let his music speak for itself. His quite unique phrasing on the accordion produces a 'lilt' and an in-built rhythm which many have tried, but failed, to reproduce. There is no flashiness in his performance and this purely reflects the man himself.

I, like many others, felt familiar with and appreciated his music for many years, but knew little about the man himself. I hope this book will give an insight to the life of this wonderful man who has given pleasure and hope to so many people.

Ian Cameron

One

At the start of the twentieth century, the dog-head shaped peninsula in Scotland known as Fife was studded with mining villages and towns. In a tenement flat in the old store buildings of one of these towns, East Wemyss, Jimmy Shand was born on 28 January 1908. No one could predict at that time that this baby, the sixth of Erskine and Mary Shand's nine children, would go on to be described during his lifetime as 'the King of Scottish Dance Music' and the most popular musician in Scottish history.

The house contained a livingroom-cum-kitchen with a cold water tap over a sink next to the coal bunker close to the window. There were two other rooms, one of which was just big enough for two beds. With such a large number of people in the house it was not unusual for two or three to use the same

Jimmy's family at his birth

3

bed and often the youngest in the family would share their parents' bed in the kitchen. The toilet was outside the house. The other children in the family were George (Dod), the eldest, Dave, Erskine, Jock, Henry, Mary (who died aged two), Kate and Nancy. Although packed together without much room or many home comforts, the Shand family were content with their situation as there were many others who lived in real poverty. The Shands had not always lived in East Wemyss but had come from Lochgelly, and for a while Erskine earned his living as a farm worker. His great love of brass band and folk music, together with his skill with a single-keyed melodeon guaranteed many tuneful times in the farm bothies as well as in the family home. After a while he changed jobs and became a pit-head contractor with responsibility for all surface workers servicing the pit. These included the operators of the cages, which carried the men down the pit shafts, and also the tumblers that tipped the coal out of the small wagons (known as hutches), onto sorting tables. The women who picked the stones out of the coal at the pit head were also answerable to Erskine Shand.

East Wemyss from the shore – Jimmy Shand's first home
(Reproduced from a Valentine postcard held in Kirkcaldy Central Library by permission of St Andrews University Library.)

Childhood days were meant for adventure, and with trees to climb, stones to throw, water to splash in and brothers and sisters to play with Jimmy made sure he did not miss out on anything that might be on offer. When the time came for him to go to school, Jimmy looked forward to it with great anticipation. The school was a tall building towering above 'the Den', a small burn with trees and bushes on its grassy banks. It had its fair mixture of good and bad teachers, some who introduced new ideas and broadened horizons, and others who followed the principle that to spare the rod was to spoil the child. Every now and then the quiet of the school day would be interrupted by the loud shouting and swearing of some parent complaining to a teacher in a neighbouring classroom. On one occasion, a mother turned up at the school with a full can of paraffin and threatened to set a teacher alight if he did not stop what was regarded as unjust persecution of her child. On the day that Jimmy was caught reading a Dixon Hawke story, he was called out to the front of the class and so savagely beaten with the tawse he fainted. (It was a week before the weals faded.) Erskine Shand was so incensed by this treatment to his son that he took time off work and made his feelings known to the school.

Jimmy managed to keep himself clear of trouble for most of his time at school, but there were others who seemed destined to fall foul of the teachers regularly. One particular school friend, far bigger than Jimmy, decided to demonstrate how independent he was on the day after he left school by turning up to shout at a teacher who had bullied him for years. 'Hah – ye'll no throw yer weight aboot noo!' he yelled, from a safe distance. The teacher's immediate response was to jump over the playground dyke and chase the boy down the road.

Jimmy followed the school routine by learning to read and write and use numbers and at the same time developed a skill in working with wood. In the evenings there was always the chance of 'a shot o dad's box', playing the melodeon. The fact that Dod could manipulate the keys, the spoon bass and the air-valve of the instrument so well made Jimmy determined to equal his older brother; so many hours were spent practising.

Outdoor activities were not neglected as it would have been a waste not to enjoy the possibilities for adventure offered by having sand, water, rocks and boats practically on the doorstep. Many a day of play ended with a crab or fish being taken home for the pot. Perhaps because of the contrast in the environment, it was the ambition of many coal face miners to have their own, or at least access to, some kind of boat. The Shands were not boat owners, but Jimmy and many of his friends spent a lot of time about the harbour, some even hoping to be asked to help fish for haddocks and codlings. 'They often as no used tae be sea-sick!' Jimmy remembers. The harbour was a safe haven for different types of boats such as yawls like *Bella-Agnes* and *Helen*, square-stern boats called *Remembrance* and *Fairy*, and a skiff named *Mermaid*. Regatta days were organised with great enthusiasm all along the Fife coast from Kinghorn to Buckhaven including Kirkcaldy, Dysart, West Wemyss and East Wemyss. These were happy family days with Regatta Queens to be chosen, many stalls to buy things from and boats decked out with fresh paint and colourful bunting. Many is the time the *Rover, Fleetwing, Barncraig, Amateur, Jim and Isabella* competed for any prizes on offer.

Model boat sailing was also very popular and some of Jimmy's friends were fortunate enough to have their own craft which they kept in fine trim. One of these friends was David Wallace, a man who came to the water regularly with his home-made 3-foot yacht. Jimmy took a special interest in this boat and when the sailing finished for the evening he would carry it back until they reached the street corner where Davie turned to go to his own house. Jimmy remembers one evening very clearly, after the model had performed particularly well.

'She fair sailed braw the nicht, Davie, the best she's ever done,' he said, feeling proud of the yacht and wishing it were his.

'Aye lauddie, it's no a bad wee boat, that it's no,' Davie replied, but when Jimmy handed the yacht to him he gave it back saying, 'Na, you keep it lauddie.'

Jimmy was now the owner of *Shamrock IV*, named after one of Sir Thomas Lipton's America's Cup yachts.

The Dookin Dub, which was a large pool cut out of the rocks, was often used for swimming. There was no need to worry about stagnant water as the tides regularly swept over the pool. Sometimes, when the weather was bad and the tides were running high, the water swamped the swimming pool and flooded part of the town.

It was not unknown for Jimmy's auntie, Phem Kerr, and her family, who lived in a house on the shore, to waken in the morning and find a foot or more of sea water inside their home. Despite all the problems the sea caused, it also provided a great source of enjoyment to Jimmy and his friends. Many's the time a group of laddies, including Davy Grant, Jim Turnbull, Jimmy Ferguson, Doug Warrender and his cousins Erskine and Tam Kerr, joined Jimmy in a game of dare against the surging waves. The idea was to sprint from the shelter of Miss Fernie's corner shop across an exposed stretch of the sea front and reach the bottom of Brewery Brae without getting wet. Timing and speed were all important to avoid being soaked by the breath-catching breakers and to be seen as one of the boys.

Jimmy Shand (centre) at eight years old, with his brother, Erskine, and sister, Nancy

Jimmy loved being by the sea, especially in the summer when the sand was warm under foot, the rocks easy to clamber over and the water pleasantly cool. One of the few things that could rival that experience was to get 'a hurl on the pug'. The 'pug' was the affectionate name given to the Wellsgreen Colliery steam engine. Sandy Hastie, the engine driver, would sometimes invite the laddies to join him on his journey from Wemyss Castle station, delivering trays of paste biscuits and sandwiches to the workers at the colliery. The paste biscuits were as filling as a meal and greatly appreciated. To be an engine driver seemed like a good idea to Jimmy and his friends. Once, when he was nine, he was offered the chance of going down the pit in the miners' transport cage but the idea frightened him. Jimmy's brother John, who was four years younger, was very happy to take his place.

Even when young, Jimmy was fond of the thought of spinning wheels and speed and longed for his own personal transport. He settled for a gird – a wonderful contraption fuelled by the imagination. A gird was a metal hoop guided and propelled by a cleek, a hand-held metal rod hooked at one end which engaged the gird low down at the rear. You could not get on a gird, you had to run along behind, but you did get the feel of controlling a mechanised vehicle. If a certain speed was not maintained the gird could wobble out of control, but with practice it could be steered very accurately round sharp corners, up and down hills and even through crowds. Many expeditions were undertaken to the next village, or even beyond, and it was a great joy to be jogging with your friends accompanying the rhythmic metallic sound of cleek on gird. Sometimes it was as if the gird had a nervous energy of its own as it bounced over the cracks and cobbles in the pavements and roads. With a gird you did not notice that your bare or sandalled feet were covering miles at a steady pace – just like the tireless heroes in the boys' papers. A gird could be anything you wanted it to be, nothing could take its place – except, maybe, a bike!

There was sometimes the chance of a shot on a pal's bike; or a pal's father's or brothers' bikes. Then of course there were your own older brothers who always seemed to get the things you desperately wanted and annoyingly kept them for themselves. Dod acquired a bike. Not just any bike; not a brakeless boneshaker without mudguards which could only be brought to a screeching, breathtaking stop by jamming the sole of your shoe against a tyre – this was a bike fit for a prince, or a

'Jimmy', complete with a bell and a pump. How Jimmy set his heart on that bike! Sometimes, he would sit in the lobby of the house admiring the ruby, twinkling, rear reflector, the brightly painted plating, the gleam of the enamel and, if nobody was around, spin the pedals listening to their quiet hum. In his mind's eye the sweep of the handlebars resembled the ears of a faithful stallion urgently waiting its master's command.

Jimmy remembers his mother calling from the kitchen: 'Come awa Jim, get awa tae the butchers noo – and hurry lauddie!' In normal circumstances he was not allowed to touch the bike but surely in such an urgent situation – 'A' richt Ma, I'm awa. I'll hurry…,' but he didn't add, '…on the bike.'

Being on the bike meant he could go the long way round to the butcher without losing any time, but it was on his road home, with the parcel of beef, that disaster struck. He was happily pedalling along, confidently controlling the bike with one hand, when a rut or unseen stone wrenched the handlebars from his grasp and he was thrown into a fence. The parcel burst open and the beef littered the dusty ground. A woman from a nearby cottage came to his aid and, after making sure he was all right, she helped him pick up the beef pieces which she washed and wrapped in fresh paper. Luckily for Jimmy the bike was not damaged and when he got home he managed to quietly sneak it into the house, but his mother was not easily fooled.

'What happened? That's no the paper the butcher uses. Did ye fa? Ye must hae. Ah, ye took the bike now didn't ye? Wait till Dod hears o this m'laud!' she said, before he could catch his breath. Jimmy was soon to find out that although melodeons could be regarded as common family property, this rule did not apply to bikes.

Jimmy did have some items of his own, one of which was his trusty 'tanner moothie'. This was a sixpenny Hohner harmonica (mouth organ) which he paid for by saving money from his part-time job at Miss Patrick's paper shop at the Black Dykes. He was seldom without this easily carried instrument and sometimes he would join his pals in an impromptu 'moothie band'. To play the harmonica you need to 'sook an blaw' to create music and this was easily compared to the melodeon's press and draw technique. There were many gifted melodeon players in the area, apart from Jimmy's father and brother Dod, which meant he had plenty of opportunities to listen and learn. On fine summer evenings Jimmy and his school pal Charlie Baillie would sit outside the Forthbank Inn and listen to Aund McAndrew, Bill Millar and other miners display their skills on the box. This inn, at 'the fit o Brewery Brae', was known locally as Tammy Hutcheson's pub. Every now and then Charlie and Jimmy would get the chance to show what they could do 'doon at the dyke' on the shore, or in the park. Their tunes would include, *Bonnie Lass o Bon Accord, Dark Lochnagar, Muckin o Geordie's Byre,* and *The 25th's Farewell to Meerut.*

On other occasions Jimmy would play with another school friend, Tam Gourdie, at an old washing-house beside the cottages at Newton Farm. It was here that Tam Nicolson, a master of the ten-key box, lived. He was a great source of inspiration and encouragement to the laddies.

On coming home from school, if he could, he would take the box out for a tune. 'Dinna be gaun faur now Jim, tea's nearly ready,' his mother would say as he went out the door. 'Jist haein a seat on the stair mither,' Jimmy replied. The curved stone walls of the spiralling inside stairwell produced an echo and amplification perfectly suited to the reedy sounds of the melodeon. This was one of his favourite practice spots which always seemed to help him produce the best of his playing ability. Often he would hear his mother's voice singing songs such as *The Auld Quarry Knowe* while she worked in the kitchen, and he would pick up the tune and accompany her on the box.

Once the day's work was done, and providing the weather was fine, Jimmy's mother, her friend Mrs Adamson and other neighbours would meet beside the little burn in The Den using a fallen tree as a seat. They proved to be an enthusiastic and knowledgeable audience as Jimmy entertained them and increased his repertoire. Although he was still a youngster he knew that a few well-selected strathspeys and reels would set their feet tapping in time with his own and even produce an occasional *Hooch!* in appreciation. Quieter tunes would include the memorable air, *The Bonnie Lass o Bon Accord*, with variations developed by the famous Scottish fiddler Scott Skinner, as well as the moving *Nameless Lassie* and the tender *Silver Threads* to which the women would softly sing the chorus: 'Darling I am growing old, Silver threads among the gold...'. Jimmy had another string to his bow, so to speak, as he had been sent for violin lessons, but he stopped these after only a year.

Apart from the moothie and the box, other music could often be heard in the Shand home by way of their most prized possession, a phonograph. With great care Jimmy would take the black cylinders from their felt-lined boxes and fit them to Thomas Edison's invention. He recalls they were, 'shiny enough tae shade yer hair in.' The family would gather round to listen to the Besses o the Barns and the Black Dyke Mills Band play inspiring marches such as *The Corinthian* and *Punchinello*. Jimmy's father, Erskine, was very enthusiastic about brass band contests and, even in the worst of weather, would travel miles to attend one. If he heard of one happening he would hurry home at midday on a Saturday, cast off his working clothes, get washed and changed and rush out the door humming 'oompah-oompah!' on his way.

It did not happen very often, but if Jimmy and his older brother Erskine did manage to have the house to themselves, they would take the chance to have their own phonograph concert. Their practised routine was to carefully lift the instrument down from the top of the chest of drawers, agree the order of playing the cylinders and Erskine would keep the motor fully wound to prevent any run down whine spoiling the music. Everything went according to plan until one day. 'G'on you an get the cylinders Jim while I wind the machine up,' said Erskine, which Jimmy duly did. Unfortunately Erskine was so preoccupied with maintaining a taut spring he overwound it. There was an ear splitting screech and the instrument and music abruptly stopped. The blue steel tension of the motive power had snapped into two shuddering distorted coils. When asked if it was ever repaired Jimmy replied, sadly, 'Na, that was it buggert for guid.'

Although the gramophone was to replace the phonograph as the most popular music player in people's homes, the Shands did not acquire one immediately. Jimmy first heard this new sound reproducer when a blind man, escorted by his daughter, visited the school and played some tunes. He was fascinated by the box and its protruding brass horn, the flat discs on a spinning turntable and the swinging arm with a needle on the end. If the pupils paid a penny they could listen to a selection of the latest records, as the thick black discs were called, such as *Abie My Boy* (*What Are You Waiting For Now?*) and *K–K–K Katie*.

Jock Allan, who with his son Jim was a very good box player, lived downstairs from the Shands and when he bought a gramophone Jimmy used to stand outside their window for hours listening to the music. The recordings included the virtuoso performances of the Hamilton mining brothers, Peter and Daniel Wyper, as well as various interpretations of traditional tunes by Jack Williams, Jimmy Brown, Peter Leatham and Palmy Dick. The *Miller of Hirn*, the *Death of Nelson* and the *High Level Hornpipe* were among Jock's favourites, so Jimmy heard them constantly and grew to like them. The Scottish, Irish, Welsh and American medleys played by Debroy Somers and the Savoy Orpheans created a great impression but the person Jimmy admired most of all was Willie Hannah, the young miner from Blackburn in West Lothian, who displayed an extensive Scots folk repertoire. Willie Hannah was, in Jimmy's words, 'A master at playin waltzes, barn dances and two-steps. I learned a lot o new tunes aff Hannah.'

Jimmy was soon to put his ability to play by ear – playing a tune without reading the music – to good use in Go-As-You-Please competitions. He remembers, 'I'd been gaein in for them since late schooldays certainly, yet before that I'd supported brither Dod at an occasional dance, and we played at picnics since I was about eleven or twelve. Oh aye, real professional –

we'd get maybe five bob for an efternoon's playing. They were maistly held in The Firs, a wood favoured by Scouts camping an the like. The outings – they werna that far out actually, a mile-an-a-half by train fae Wemyss Castle station tae West Wemyss. Anyway, we would be playing for the lassies fae the Linen Factory an their lads maistly. The folk fair enjoyed theirsel's – races, rounders, hackie-duck, dancing on the grass. The one drawback was the midges – I used tae suffer for weeks efter, they got a rare chance at ye when yer hands were busy playin – but happy days, aye, happy days.' Events like these were useful in getting used to facing an audience, something he found very difficult. 'Shy then? I've aye been shy, an shy yet. I would look tae one side, or at the grund – anyplace but at a' they folk lookin at me!'

When the Shands did get their own gramophone there were several popular recording companies such as Regal, HMV, Zonophone, Winner and Columbia producing a wide range of music. They also had the good sense to identify their productions with different coloured labels. There was a strike in 1921 and, although he was only thirteen, Jimmy was asked to play with Johnny Hope at fund-raising dances and benefit concerts. By now he had his own bike which was put to good use, taking him to various parts of the county. The first bike Jimmy's father bought him was a bargain, even for those days. It cost half-a-crown and had a back-pedalling brake and Jimmy was very proud of it.

Jimmy left school in April 1922 aged fourteen and, given his choice, he would have continued his interest in making things with wood by becoming an apprentice joiner. The prospects of an apprenticeship in any trade were not very bright, especially in a small town, but there was one area of employment which was always looking for laddies… the mining industry. Putting aside his earlier reluctance five years before to go down a pit, Jimmy determined to make the best of things to earn a living.

Mary Shand was up early in the morning of Jimmy's first day at work. She laid out his sark, a blue flannel shirt, checked his boots were tacketed completely from heel-tip to toe and proudly brushed down his new moleskin trousers, making sure they had their own knee strings to make nicky-tams. These were made by tying the string below the knee and lifting a space of trouser above to allow for bending and kneeling. More practical or sensible working trousers would have been hard to find.

By 4.30 Jimmy was on his way, his boots striking sparks off the road as he walked the mile-and-a-half to Lochhead Pit. It was a fine spring morning and the birds were singing hard to welcome the daylight as Jimmy checked that his piece-box and water-filled flask were intact. 'A jeely piece and sup o cauld water doon below – nae steak wi trimmins since has ever equalled it,' Jimmy recalls.

Stepping into the cage and dropping down the pit shaft was a strange sensation, as half way down it felt as if everything was coming back up. Even when the bottom was reached there was still a long walk 'doon the dook' before anyone reached the point where they could start earning money. Jimmy's job was coupling-on, linking the hutches (little wagons) which carried the coal from the face. This was hard work, moving two and sometimes three hutches at a time, and Jimmy soon developed powerful leg muscles. The wages for these efforts was 3/6d a day.

The Maintenance/Roadman down the pit, old Geordie Drylie, mentioned to Jimmy that his son Davie, who worked at Lochhead Mine, needed a laddie. After three weeks going down a pit, Jimmy left to go down a mine. Strange though it may seem there was a difference. To enter a pit, you drop down a shaft in a lift cage; a mine is entered by walking or riding down a slope (this was known as surface-dipping). At Lochhead they rode in on hutches. There were three 'races' (a string of twelve hutches with four men in each) operating. It was better for the laddies to be in the first or second race as the men did not like to be kept waiting. Each morning the unforgettable stench of foul air had to be overcome as it came belching through behind the wooden trap which was opened to let the hutches in. There was no getting away from the dank, unpleasant atmosphere.

Jimmy's job in the mine was drawing and filling, which meant shovelling out and loading onto hutches, coal that Davy Drylie hacked out while crouching at the work face. The colliers were paid by the company for the tonnage they mined and they in turn paid the laddies. This meant that Jimmy earned an extra bob a day. He soon found out that if he could keep up with another collier he could earn more money. Jimmy worked hard and he was soon coping with the output of three men (Tam Foster, Willie Logie and Watt Pryde) and earning more than 7/6d a day.

He liked the work, and the money was good and it meant that he could move on from being a push-bike owner to being a motorbike owner. Jimmy's first motorbike was even cheaper than his first push-bike. It was a free gift from Jock Brand, the lad who was courting his sister, Nancy. Jimmy took his pal Tam Gourdie with him to help wheel it home the four miles from Leven. He was quite proud of his 1921 Diamond with belt-driven 2½ horse power J.A.P. engine, registration number SG 301.

Despite the long hours at work, Jimmy did not neglect practising on his box; as he said, 'Of coorse I kept at it – after my shift doon the mine – a tune or twa every day.' The pattern of Jimmy's life seemed settled until one day, in 1926, the miners were locked out. This action by the mine owners was not totally unexpected but it still came as a shock. For over a year the Government had been paying the owners a subsidy on the tonnage mined, but when this was withdrawn the miners were asked to take a cut in wages. This they refused to do and they were locked out. In support of the miners the Trades Union Congress called for a general strike which started on 4 May 1926. The general feeling among the workers was that they would soon be back at work so why not make the best of the break while the weather was fine. By now Jimmy owned an International 19 Key 4 Spoon Bass and Air Valve melodeon, which his Aunt Grace had given him, and he felt well equipped to travel round the country and coastal towns and villages that advertised Go-As-You-Please competitions. The experience of playing in front of an audience was worthwhile on its own but Jimmy did not object if he also picked up ten bob as a first prize.

The general strike lasted nine days, but the miners stayed locked out and once any savings they might have tucked away had been used, the men and their families experienced great hardship. Jimmy was very aware of the situation, as more than once he found his mother in tears as she could not 'pey her shop' (she did not have the money to settle the grocery bill at the Co-op). The Co-operative Society cannot be praised highly enough for the way it provided a lifeline to so many families at this time. The local management and the national organisation displayed great patience and understanding, and demonstrated their belief that, when the women had money in their purses again, they would start to pay off the back-log of credit that had built up over the weeks and months.

Although they were unemployed, the miners were not idle, as they spent a great deal of time organising soup-kitchens and fund-raising events. Much of the money for the soup-kitchens was gathered by groups of miner-musicians, including Jimmy, wandering from town to town busking for coppers in the gutter. Jimmy remembers they even went as far as Dundee on the other side of the Firth of Tay. He also played at strike dances at Denbeath Institute with his friend Bob McArtney vamping on the piano. At this time the only regular money coming into the Shand household was the little over £2 a week that Jimmy's brother Erskine earned driving a horse and cart.

One afternoon when 'oot for a choon' on Level Links, Jimmy met up with someone who was to become a great friend. This was Johnny McDill, a skilled box player, who was more than half blind following a gas attack during the 1914–18 war. He had trained as a poultry keeper and a grant enabled him to run a small poultry farm near New Gilston at Woodside. This ensured he had a regular income and food on the table, which was more than most families could claim.

Regardless of all the difficulties, folk always seemed to do something special for a wedding and certainly the celebrations would not be complete without music. Many's the time Jimmy was happy to play for an agreed fee – a free meal! On some occasions Johnny McDill would play alongside him and the range of music they produced included *Petronella, Strip the Willow* and *Rory o More* as well as quadrilles, lancers, schottische and the Circle Waltz.

Jimmy soon discovered that Johnny was an expert on the workings of the melodeon, despite his poor eyesight, and he took great pleasure in teaching Jimmy all he knew about taking the instrument apart to repair, to retune and re-assemble. Jimmy acknowledged he was forever grateful to be taught these skills.

In August 1926 the miners went back to work out of desperation and accepted the reduced wages they had rejected earlier in the year. It was a period of severe economic depression and unemployment and there were not enough jobs for everyone. Jimmy decided he did not want to go back down the mine and sought out other ways to earn a living.

Two

Working as a navvy on a waterworks scheme near Pittenweem was the first job Jimmy managed to get after the strike was over. This was hard work – shovelling puddle-clay which was used to build the banking round the reservoir – but Jimmy did not complain as he was glad to be earning some money. Unfortunately the work available only lasted for a few months at a time and was normally followed by longer periods of unemployment. Jimmy recalls that folk considered themselves fortunate if they had three months' work in a year. In the meantime Dod had taken the initiative and set himself up in business, and when he obtained his first order he asked Jimmy to work with him. They had a contract with the Denbeath and Michael Collieries to manufacture concrete blocks, which involved a great deal of hard work. They had to unload all their own stone chips and cement and, as they were on piece work, they could hardly catch their breath or take time off. Sometimes it was, literally, very difficult to take a breath as a lot of the work was done in a shed with no ventilation. Inside, they kept a coal fire burning for the benefit of the cement, and had to be nearly asphyxiated before they would open the door.

The brothers had so much work at the Denbeath Colliery they decided to bring in Geordie Denham, an ex-miner, to help. This was to benefit the Shands in more ways than they thought possible. Geordie had the habit of going home for something to eat at lunch time, and one day he said, 'Mither, they twa lauds hae tae sit there wi jist a dry piece.' Mrs Denham looked up and said, 'Bring them hame efter this then, anither plate o soup's neither here nor there.' In no time at all the Denham family and the Shands became firm friends.

When the contract at the Michael ended, Jimmy went on his own to do the same sort of work at Stirling, and when that finished, at High Valleyfield. In the evenings he took as many playing engagements as he could get, such as wedding sprees or Miners Institute Dances, travelling to them by motorbike, if it was working. It was a proud day when he was able to buy a second-hand New Imperial, 1922, with a 2¾ hp. J.A.P. engine for £16 from Alec Allan.

Although motorbikes were good value, most of them normally had poor front brakes, a fact which had not escaped the notice of the police and it was not unusual for motor-cyclists to be stopped for spot checks. On the day he bought the bike, Jimmy wheeled it to the nearest petrol pump, filled the tank, got on, drove off and was stopped immediately. Within an hour of owning the bike he was booked for having faulty brakes and subsequently had to pay a fine.

Just as he had found it useful to know about the construction of a melodeon, Jimmy was soon convinced he needed to be aware of the mechanics of motorbikes. Of course, he had many pals who claimed to be experts and who talked over his head, using highly technical expressions such as 'piston rings' and 'de-carbonisation'. This seemingly magic circle included Wull Whyte, Eck Horsburgh and Sandy Laing. There was obviously only one thing for it, he was assured, he needed to change his piston rings. After buying a new set, Jimmy and the experts gathered one Sunday morning to perform the operation. On this occasion the opportunity was taken to provide an instructive tutorial on the internal combustion engine and how to maintain it. It was important to impress Jimmy, so everything was done with dramatic gestures. After the old piston rings were removed they were passed round for comment on their worn condition, pulled apart to show how fragile they were, and then tossed aside with a flourish. The next stage in the procedure was to fit the new rings – which promptly broke! Jimmy certainly remembered that day. As he said, 'Aye, a lesson I've never forgotten – *leave well alone!*'

On many of his motorbike trips to fulfil playing engagements, Jimmy had Johnny McDill on the pillion seat. Johnny's poor vision meant he was thankfully unaware of the many hair-raising situations that Jimmy managed to scramble through on the journeys. Returning home one dark night they sped round a tight bend. 'Goad man Jim, it's a bloody rough road this,' Johnny shouted, desperately hanging on at the back. 'Aye, 'tis that,' Jimmy replied as he battled to get the motorbike down from the bank it was speeding along, and back onto the road!

There was another dark night when a drunk man staggered in front of them and fell to the ground. Jimmy immediately went to the man's aid and, as he anxiously bent over him, he realised the man's coat was wet. Was it blood? Thankfully no – the man had been carrying a half-bottle of rum in his pocket and this had broken when he fell.

Ice and snow were extra hazards during the winter, and Jimmy found it easier to move into digs nearer to wherever he happened to be working. He remembers being very contented with landladies such as Mrs Hogg of Fallin in Stirling, Mrs Nicoll of High Valleyfield and a lady who was a niece of Johnny McDill's, Mrs Lamont at Cairneyhill. Another landlady made a lasting impression on Jimmy – mainly because of her soup. 'Jist lumps o half-raw vegetables floatin in hot water. Every nicht the stuff was set doon in a big plate, aye gien a different name but aye the same – tae me anyway – unpalatable slap.' "Plenty mair now," she would say. "My, ye're slow compared tae my man – he'd hae haen at least three platefus by noo!"' Jimmy continues: 'Up until then I never was awfy keen on soup, yet, strangely enough, this wife's cookin – or semi-cookin – instead o pittin me aff it a'thegither for life gied me a taste for it. No for hers – but an appreciation o my mither's makin when I went hame at a weekend!'

While the rest of the family travelled to wherever the work was, Jimmy's sister Nancy always stayed at home to help their mother. This was by no means an easy option for a house proud lass. For years she fought a losing battle to get her father and brothers to take off their heavy boots at the doorway. Then there was the washing ritual of the men themselves, where she was involved in a great deal of heavy work filling the pots and big black kettles with water to be heated on the range. The steaming containers then had to be carefully carried and emptied into a large tin bath. What with the washing, the cooking and the cleaning of the house, to say nothing of the endless task of black-leading the range, she must have wished at times she had gone out to work. She was sharing the household load when her mother died.

Mrs Mary Shand was fifty two years old when she died in 1929. She had devoted her life to bringing up and looking after her family, and no matter how bad some times were, she always managed to find a cup of tea for any stranger who came to the door. On the night his mother died, twenty-one year old Jimmy wandered down to the shore with memories flooding through his mind. He thought of the times he played the box on the stair, and for his mother and her friends in The Den, and a particular tune ran through his mind *Lay My Head Beneath A Rose*. He also recalled, as he sat on the dyke watching the full moon reflected on the water, that only once had her trusting nature been betrayed. It was a regular practice to allow wandering down-and-outs to take the chill out of their bones by letting them sleep over the boilers at the mine where Erskine Shand worked. 'Whar's yer braw cords the day, Mr Shand?' asked one of the dossers, referring to the brand new pair of trousers he had seen worn for the first time the previous day. 'Oh, they got weet yesterday – left them aff tae get richt dry,' was the reply. On hearing this, the vagabond went down to the house and said, 'Mrs Shand, yer man sent me doon for his new corduroys, he's decided tae wear them efter a'.' Needless to say, Erskine Shand was never to see or wear them again. Despite this experience, no one was ever turned away from Mary Shand's door.

After his mother's death, Jimmy's sister Nancy continued to look after the family until she got married to John Brand, a moulder in Balfour's Foundry. After the wedding they moved to Leven and Aunt Rachel, a former pit-head worker, took over as housekeeper, proving to be a very good friend and support to the Shands.

Work was still not easy to find and sometimes involved travelling all over the country. It was a little easier if the motorbike was working, but when it was out of action Jimmy had to use a push-bike. A round trip of over thirty miles a day on the bike was not unusual. What these, sometimes short, spells of employment meant to Jimmy was experience as well as money. In some cases the experience could be used in various situations, but in others the skills were lost when the employment ended.

Jimmy managed to get some work with Robert Terras, a building contractor, and while he was there the chance of working with a hod arose. He was very keen to do this as he could earn even more money this way. Hod carrying was not as easy as it sounds as it required not only strength, which Jimmy certainly had, but a particular knack, which he worked hard to acquire. To carry a fully loaded hod successfully needed a certain balancing skill, and until this became second nature Jimmy had many a frustrating and exhausting time. Eventually the knack came and he confidently navigated his way round the building site and up and down ladders, whistling cheerfully some favourite tune. Then he was paid off and the new skill was wasted.

The prospects for good permanent daytime work had not improved but there were more opportunities on the musical front in the evenings and weekends. If he were lucky, Jimmy would get paid a small fee, but at other times he would simply earn his supper. Jimmy regarded all of these occasions as an opportunity to improve his playing and would get great satisfaction if he felt he had made a significant difference in his interpretation of a waltz, a hornpipe or a schottische. The many Go-As-You-Please contests being held all over Fife offered a quick way to find out what the public thought of his playing. These contests were held in schools, cinemas, theatres and large as well as small village halls. The rules were very simple: the prizes, which were normally no more than ten shillings, were awarded to the contestants who received the most applause. Jimmy did very well in these contests, but his most vivid memory of these occasions is not one of his successes but of an old busker who wandered round the villages and towns producing some terrible sounds from an old battered concertina. At Green's Playhouse in Leven they were in the same contest. The busker's playing had not improved and the high pitched screeches were greeted by loud foot-stamping, earthy shouts and cheers and derisive slow hand-clapping from the audience. Thinking he was getting a wonderful reception he kept going with great gusto. Based on the volume of the audience response he should have been an easy winner, at least that was the theory. As Jimmy remembers, 'He took some dragging off.'

Most towns had their buskers, many of them worn out through years of war and want, some trying to retain some sort of dignity by going through the motions of earning a living. The genuine ones considered themselves entertainers and gave of their best. Everything from *When You Played The Organ And I Sang The Rosary* to *The Old Rugged Cross* and *The Nicht I Took Big Aggie To The Ball* were attempted by singers with fine voices, and others with no voice at all. Mouth organs were sucked and blown to the detriment of any tune, little melody was scraped out of ancient fiddles and breathless people attempted to produce jaunty airs on tin whistles. Others with mandolin or plectrumed banjo attacked tunes such as *Way Down Upon The Swanee River, Marching Through Georgia* and *Camptown Races.* Sometimes only the *Doo-da-doo-da-day, Plonk!* of the final song sounded as it should. There were, of course, some performers whose skill would have graced any stage.

There was a wide range of different types of melodeons played by the travelling musicians. Some had survived being played by generations of relatives in farm bothy breaks, while others had a variety of combinations of keys and bass. Every now and then a player would appear with a swanky imported Italian box with piano keys. It is probable that these had been bought on credit in easier times, and their owners were now vamping like mad renderings of *Lady of Spain* and *Valencia* to keep them out of the pawn shop.

Jimmy had never really been a busker, except when he travelled round Fife and went as far as Dundee to raise money for soup kitchens during the miners' strike. This experience gave him an insight into, and a sympathy for, the busker's way of life which he quickly decided was not for him. He remembers one occasion in which a wandering piper played a prominent part.

'This piper was what ye would cry an economical busker – aimed tae play only where he was pretty sure o gettin somethin. Well, I was up in the hoose o a pal in New Gilston, Sandy Laing, haein a cup o tea wi them when the piper obliged wi a tune ootside and was invited in. Then he spots Mrs Laing's married dochter on a visit fae her hoose at the foot o the road – a lass as guid-herted as her mither. "Oh, so this is whar ye are!" cries the piper in what could've been mock indignation. "An me blawin ma guts oot doonby at yer door!" He was surprised when I said, "Sit doon Arthur, an gies yer crack." I'd kent him as a pony driver doon the mine.'

Jimmy realised that, although he could earn a few shillings playing for hours at weddings, dances and sprees, he could not make enough to live off. The work was not regular and there were too many musicians willing to take up the engagements. If he was lucky enough to have a labouring job he kept at it for as long as it lasted. He was to dig so many trenches that he felt at times he was starting a new pit shaft. In all weathers, in all seasons, he could be wielding a shovel, swinging a pick, pushing a barrow or grappling with an obstinate rock.

Getting to and from work could be a hazardous adventure on its own. Some of the roads in Fife were narrow, twisting, switch-backed ribbons of tarmacadam, which demanded foresight, restraint and sometimes hair-trigger reactions from Jimmy, the speed king of the motorbike. One of the problems was the rival bus companies in their attempts to beat each other to the stops. In one district, a tram company and two bus companies were in direct competition. Timetables were often abandoned as they strove to pick up passengers before their rivals. Of course, those members of the public who used public

transport were happy with the choice, but the other users of the
meandering roads had to be wary. It was not unusual for a
motor cyclist or a motorist to approach a bend and suddenly
find not just one but two buses charging neck and neck
towards them.

Jimmy remembers visiting Doug Warrender, an old school
pal, whose wife Lizzie was a clippie, a bus conductress. Lizzie,
who came from Buckhaven (*Buckhind* the locals called it)
recalled: 'Aye, we'd tae work for oor money, thae days. Three
buses I'd tae conduct then, dashing fae and tae the ither when
they drew up. The drivers werna keen at a' on drawin up – get
on, get on, was their idea. It was nothing for them tae leave the
route a'thegither tae flee doon a side road for a shoart cut tae
beat the ither buses. An the last buses! I've had them sittin on
the mudgairds! Wages? Thirty shillings a week – aye, an let ye
miss twa fares an ye were liable tae get twa days suspension!'

At the same time as Lizzie was sweeping through Fife, in a
uniform that could have been made for the Keystone Cops,
Doug was working equally hard on building sites laying as
many as 240–250 bricks an hour. At the talk of the possibility of
any bonus some old timers would laugh and say, 'Lucky tae be
workin at a', lauddie!'

By the time Jimmy was twenty-five a certain routine seemed
to have developed in his life. He would work hard during the
day, if he were lucky enough to be in employment, and he
found time to play his box in the evenings and weekends. This
was soon to change when, early in 1933, his father Erskine died.
As he lay in bed, surrounded by his family, Erskine spent his
last few hours reliving a lifetime of hard work. He recalled, in
graphic detail, his first job as a farm lad and of how the various
seasons affected the type of work he did. He remembered, with
affection, the many grieves he had known and the merits of
some farm horses. He laughed as he talked of the happy nights
in the bothies when the entertainment was provided by fiddle
and melodeon. He seemed to once more take charge at the pit-
head and lamented the days of the lock out. The days of
hardship were recalled before revealing the pride he felt on

what he had done in his final job as a roadman. He died on a Sunday, the traditional day of rest, in the house he had brought his family up in. Jimmy recalls several incidents that occurred when his father was a roadman looking after a four-mile stretch near East Wemyss. Not for the first time, the big hollow on the outskirts of Rosie village had flooded and, as before, Erskine had waded through the muddy ditches, waist deep in water to clear the drain. The second incident involved a tar boiler which had been parked outside the old store buildings to enable road repairs to start the next day. Erskine's job was to ensure that the tar was melted in readiness, therefore he stoked the boiler last thing at night. Unfortunately, a strong wind got up during the night and the tar caught fire. There was great confusion and the fire brigade had to be called out. Next day, at work, Erskine collapsed and was pronounced dead by a policeman and several other people. However, if it had not been for neighbour Lou Adamson's wife, who kept massaging his heart until it restarted, he would not have survived.

A few months later Jimmy's fame as a box player was such he was granted what seemed like his big chance: an audition with the BBC. At the time, Jimmy thought how proud his father would have been to know it. However, the audition was not a success. The reason the BBC gave for turning Jimmy down was – *he kept time with his foot!* Confident there was nothing wrong with his music, Jimmy kept playing his box.

The Denham family, who had been so kind to the Shand brothers during their block-making days, had moved to Dundee and Jimmy visited them some weekends. Geordie had moved to Edinburgh to work in the Café Royal. He had made himself look older and more experienced at the interview by borrowing a sophisticated hat to wear. With the job prospects in and around East Wemyss being so poor, Jimmy decided to investigate the possibility of any casual labouring work in Dundee. He had been unemployed for so long he was forced to go on the Means Test, a scheme that totalled all the money going into a household and insisted that those family members fortunate enough to be in employment had to support any others out of work. To ensure that this was stringently enforced, the Government employed an army of professional snoopers, but often accepted information from spiteful, unpaid, informers. This malicious test destroyed many a family, as the only way the unemployed could get any benefits was when their working brothers and sisters moved out into lodgings. Sometimes this could mean going to another town or a different part of the country, depending on the work.

When in Dundee Jimmy often went for a stroll round the town with 'uncle' Jim Denham. Each time they would stop and look at the enticing display of accordions in the windows of J.T. Forbes' music shop in King Street. Eventually, on being assured it wouldn't cost him anything to try one, Jimmy was persuaded to enter the shop. Once on the premises he was introduced to Charles S. Forbes who listened to him play a few tunes and promptly offered him a job.

Although flattered, Jimmy took his time to consider his options. What would the job be? Would he be a shop assistant or a sales rep? Certainly the thought of spending his days among accordions of all sizes, shapes and prices interested him, as did the fact he would be expected to drive the Forbes' wee yellow van. Would he, a labourer all his working life, be able to cope with what was being proposed? He was continually being told that his virtuosity would soon receive the proper recognition and acclaim it deserved. Jimmy was not so sure but he was canny enough to see he should keep on friendly terms with Charles S. Forbes. As he put it himself, 'It's no *what* ye ken, it's *wha* ye ken!'

Forbes, who had contacts in London, was convinced that Jimmy was good enough to interest a record company. Jimmy, on the other hand, although he knew that Forbes's opinion was respected in the music world, remembered his own BBC experience and had little faith that very much could be done for him. It was better not to build up one's hopes about the possibilities of making a record, as probably nothing would come of it. Anyway, Jimmy had been offered a job, laying cable at Abercrombie Farm for the Fife Power Company. Charles Forbes was not easily discouraged and looked forward to Jimmy's visits to his shop. In the autumn of 1933, diddling (a form of mouth music), fiddling and melodeon contests were held regularly in the villages round about Dundee, and Forbes persuaded Jimmy to enter one at Alyth. As the venue was about seventeen miles north of Dundee, Forbes suggested to Jimmy, 'I'll run you out and back, of course,' adding 'come up to the house for your tea first – the wife would like to hear you playing.'

These contests were always well attended, as there was a great pool of talent in the county of Angus. Another competitor at Alyth who had been offered a lift was lorry driver Wull Kydd. Wull, a regular prize winner brimming full of confidence, apparently had gone into Forbes' shop, played his competition selection and said, 'Well see if this Shand ye think sae much o can beat *that*, Mr Forbes!'

On the night of the contest, after he had finished his tea in the Forbes house in Shamrock Street, Jimmy strapped on his box and played a few tunes for Mrs Forbes. At the same time, outside the house, Wull Kydd stopped – and listened. He listened with an experienced ear until the last faultless chord ended, hesitated for a few moments and then knocked the door. Once inside, he stated he had seriously considered turning back as he could see no point in competing against someone of Jimmy's calibre.

Later that evening, in Alyth, the first prize – worth £3 and the offer to make a record with the Great Scot Company (of Drummond, Megginch) – was won by Davie Raitt, the well known footballer–accordionist. Jimmy was second with the march, strathspey and reel, *Inverness Gathering*, *Braes o Tulliment* and *John Cheap the Chapman*. The third prize went to Will Powrie, a grieve from near Blairgowrie. This meeting was the start of a long-standing friendship with the Powrie family.

Jimmy was presented with a chromium-plated cake stand as his prize but as the judges had been so impressed by the brilliance of his performance he too was offered the chance to

make a record. He declined, as a short time before, Charles
Forbes had given him a letter stating that Regal–Zonophone,
the celebrated recording company of London, wanted him to
record for them. Jimmy was under the impression at the time
that Charles Forbes had convinced Regal–Zonophone to take a
chance with the recording session. He did not know that Forbes
had guaranteed to cover the costs if the venture was
unsuccessful. Jimmy remembers the recording experience very
clearly.

'I went doon tae London – kind o feard as you would say.
Nae knowledge – nae nothin. I could play a tune or twa but
that was aboot a'. Went into this big studio, Abbey Road in
London, still in operation the day – I felt strange goin in there
wi ma wee melodeon. The arrangement was they were to
provide a pianist tae play for me. Well they did, a really good
one at that, but I didna ken enough aboot music to let the man
know the kind o rhythm I wanted. Nae idea – and I was to
make three records. Well, I mind I tried the piano for the first
ane – it wisna very good, coudna get goin at a'. However, we
made two sides an then I asked if I coudna dae the other four
sides masel – by this time I was aboot played sick. I had been
playin thro tryin to get the man into the theme o the thing but
nae idea – I coudna help him.'

Three records were made although only two were issued
because of technical difficulties – they were the two without the
pianist. The tunes were *Drunken Piper, Laird o Dunblair, De'il
Amang the Tailors, Punchbowl, Fair Maid of Perth,* and the *Atholl
Gathering, Rakes o' Kildare, Teviot Bridge* plus *Londonderry* and
High Level hornpipes. This was the only recording of the last
two tunes that Jimmy made.

All this time Jimmy still had his day job laying cables in Fife,
although he was considering other prospects. A comment came
to mind – made by a smith known as old Pebbles, who Jimmy
sometimes visited in the evening after working at Pittenweem
reservoir. 'Mmm, aye lauddie, thae hauns are never meant for
hard work!' When he remembered that, since he had left
school, his hands had been used to push and drag hutches

along narrow tracks in cramped tunnels while he was bent over like a half-shut knife; and how, after the lock out, they were used for pulling barrows, swinging picks and lifting bricks among other things, Jimmy smiled to himself. Old Peebles could not have been more wrong.

Others found it hard to believe that such abused hands and fingers could persuade air and reeds to render tunes such as *The Auld Hoose* in such a way as to bring sentimental tears to the eyes of the toughest of men. As more and more people were becoming aware of his music, Jimmy decided on a positive change in his life style.

About this time the newspapers printed an appeal to help provide Christmas cheer at the Dundee Royal Infirmary. The appeal read:

> If we have gramophone records that do us good to listen to, let us send them to our ailing folks who have much more need of being enlivened and encouraged. If we don't have gramophone records let us buy one, two, three or four at 1/11d or 7/6d, with the chance that some bit of music or humour will, by the real magic that works better than some medicine, put some downcast invalid in the mood that brings back good health… The gramophone records contributed almost two years ago are worn out. No one can know the good they did, the cures they wrought.

Jimmy could not donate anything at this time, as his Regal–Zonophone records were not yet issued, but he did consider the power and influence of music.

His last navvying job was in Fife. By Christmas 1933 he had agreed to work for Charles Forbes. The possibility of driving the company's bright yellow Austin 10 van had nothing to do with it, of course! There was no problem in finding accommodation in Dundee – he moved into 185 Princes Street to lodge with Geordie Denham's mother.

Three

Mrs Denham was not sure it was a good idea for Jimmy to lodge in her house. It was not that she did not like him; indeed, it was out of concern for him that she said he should possibly consider living with one or other of his aunts who lived in Dundee. Her main worry was for him 'in this hoose fu o bairns. There's no much peace here for anybody?' The busy household was exactly what Jimmy wanted, and as his pal George was not home very often he moved into his room. Jimmy thought the Denham bairns were wonderful and they in turn enjoyed having him around.

Times were hard, very hard. To help generate some extra money Mrs Denham cooked potted hough and baked cakes, which her husband Will loaded on to bakers' boards and sold round the streets. A hundred bowls of potted hough were produced in each batch and sold at 3d a time.

The Denham family always had time to help others. Following the gramophone record appeal, more than 1,500 records were collected, mostly by Stevenson's Laundry van drivers in their spare time. One of the volunteer drivers was 'uncle' Jim Denham.

'Bonnie' Dundee was not a very apt description of the city in the early thirties. When most people thought of Dundee, they thought of jute, jam and journalism. In 1933 there was very little jam to go round and most of the journalists were writing depressing stories about the jute industry, the major employer in the city. The economy of Dundee depended heavily on a busy and prosperous jute industry, but as half of the 34,000 jute workers were unemployed, many families suffered real hardship. Imports of raw jute were down by 100,000 tons compared to the trade before the First World War.

The ironical thing is that there was no drop in the demand

for jute products; it was simply that this demand was being met by the increase in the importation of cheap jute cloth from India. Investment in India, including jute-spinning machinery, since the middle of the 19th century, coupled with the easy access to raw material and cheap labour, contributed to the many thousands on the dole in Dundee.

Before Jimmy moved to the city, the unemployed had sent a deputation to the Town Council asking for promises that the dependants of anyone who went on a hunger march to London would not suffer by having their benefits cut or delayed. There were nation-wide protests about a new Unemployment Bill.

As an indication of how out of touch some of the better off in society were about the desperate plight of the poor, one well-known lady stated that all people needed to do was introduce wiser household management. She then proceeded to com-pound her ignorance by pontificating on how to make a pot of soup for 2d. It had not occurred to her that economic necessity had already forced generations of housewives to become wizards in the frugal topping-up of the kail pot.

If families saw meat at all it was usually in a stew made from unidentifiable left over scraps or cuttings. Some butchers in the poorer districts promoted their wares with the slogan: 'Come in and buy or we'll both starve.' To help sales they offered shilling parcels – a sausage or two, a bit of mince, perhaps a chop – depending on what was available and would not keep much longer. Stovies were a cheap and popular meal made from potatoes, onions and a lump of fat cooked in the minimum of water until brown – greasy, but satisfying.

The experienced shoppers knew the best places to be and when to be there to get good value. One place was the down-town greenmarket last minute on a Saturday evening. There was always the chance of picking up bargains in fruit, vegetables and beef from the open air stalls, as the owners were keen to get home. There was also the extra attraction of being entertained by two well known Dundee minstrels, Paddy McGrory and Blind Mattie.

Mattie, although she accompanied herself on a simple box,

depended on her voice more than her playing to entertain the crowds. Paddy, whose busking always attracted large numbers, had reputedly once been declared the Scottish Champion Melodeon Player. The story goes that Paddy reached the final of a competition playing his comparatively unpretentious box. The co-finalist was an Italian, playing an expensive piano accordion. The judges could not decide who was the winner after listening to both of them play tune after tune. It was suggested they swap instruments, which they did. The Italian could not make head nor tail of the button keys, but Paddy produced a tune which won him the award. (The title of Scottish Champion Accordionist had been conferred on William Hannah in promotional material for Wilkinson's Excelsior which referred to five different models, steel reeds, tuned to British Chromatic Extended Scale.)

Jimmy started work at Forbes' for 35 shillings a week. He paid 25 shillings for board and lodging each week and 5 shillings towards the price of a £33 two-row bass box: he was left with 2s. 8½d after the price of a stamp was deducted. A regular offer of professional engagements began to come his way, and in some he could earn as much as fifteen bob for a night's playing, which was very welcome, but could mean playing on the box all night. Sometimes wee Isa Denham would come rushing in from Butterburn School and Jimmy would say, 'Clean my shoes, hen, an I'll gie ye thruppence,' as he would be playing that night. 'See an dae the insteps properly an a',' he would add, as he liked things just right. Mrs Denham would iron his shirt and he would set off spick and span and feel king of the walk.

Isa was between seven and eight years old when Jimmy moved into the house and she remembers he always seemed to be hearing tunes; he was always humming and drumming his fingers on the arm of his chair. This was an old hard wooden armchair which was situated between the kitchen sink and the fireplace. There was one occasion when Will Fyffe, the famous Scottish entertainer, was appearing in *Babes in the Wood* at the Kings Theatre. This prompted the Denhams to stage their own 'panto'. Jimmy would say, 'C'mon, let's hae a concert!' Isa would put a stick under her arm, don an old hat of her Dad's and do the cake walk dance. Wee Jim Denham would do his Tarzan act by stripping off and wrapping his mother's fox fur round him. His special trick was to issue a blood-curdling yell and take a flying leap from the bunker. Everybody sang and danced but there was one song which was very popular:

> If you should see a bit fat wumman
> Standin at the closie bummin
> That's ma Ma-a-am-mee!

The Denhams' house was on the top pletty. Pletties were the long iron-railed stone platforms which served the storeys of the old tenements connected by an outside stair. They overlooked a big square of back greens behind the tenements in Arbroath Road, Robertson Street and Graham Place in Dundee. All Jimmy had to do was step out of the door with his melodeon and people would appear on the other pletties. When he started to play they not only listened and danced, but called across in the music breaks for this strathspey or that reel. In the tenements with no pletties, but inside stairs, the windows were raised and people could be seen birling past, the arms linked with their neighbours. Every now and then there would be a loud *hooch!*; it was not unusual to see the windows of the toilets on the outside stairs opening to let people listen while they were otherwise occupied. Despite the very hard times, most people still seemed to have a joy, a lightness in their souls which just needed to be awakened – Jimmy and his music was able to do that.

Shortly after starting with Forbes, Jimmy spoke about the possibility of producing an accordion with more bass and treble keys. Charles Forbes agreed to send an order to Hohner, the German accordion manufacturer, if Jimmy could supply specifications. Jimmy asked for an instrument with 34 treble keys – British Chromatic (with three sets of reeds, tremolo tuned) – and 80 bass. The order was completed and arrived in the middle of 1934 and was called a 'L'Organola' with a grey pearloid finish. Hohner had given it a brand name used for their range of piano accordions.

The night that Jimmy first appeared at the Plaza in Hilltown was not just a great occasion for him, it was a proud night for the Denhams. The whole family turned up, even Gran and Grandad, who had come in especially from Longforgan. Mrs Denham had a battle on her hands persuading Jimmy to wear the fancy purple satin Cossack blouse, which had been provided for the occasion by the promoter of the evening. Eventually, he was all dolled up standing on the stage, shaking his head in annoyance at the bright spotlight trained on him. At one point he stopped and refused to continue his recital until the brightness was reduced.

Very soon the name and fame of Jimmy Shand spread beyond Dundee, across to the west coast, up north and down south into England. Charles Forbes was not slow to recognise the value of his employee. He travelled around selling his wares while Jimmy demonstrated the boxes in halls large and small. Ever the businessman, Forbes advertised a minimal charge of 6d to hear Jimmy play!

They went as far south as Lockerbie and Yetholm, calling at most towns in between. One time, at Boarhills near St Andrews, Charles Forbes was ill and the shy Jimmy had to lecture as well as play. 'Mind you,' he recalls, 'there was a lot mair playin than talkin!'

Jimmy did not have a flashy or flourishing style, and many people commented that no other player ever got so much out the accordion with such a minimum movement of the bellows. After one demonstration in Peebles, a round-eyed little girl said to her mum, 'The man just came oot, and just stood, and the music came itself!'

When he was not touring Jimmy demonstrated in the shop to potential customers and followed up enquiries. One part of his job he didn't like was having occasionally to go debt collecting, as he had known hardship and how devastating it could be.

Things were beginning to get better for Jimmy, as his basic

pay could be enhanced with commission. The rates were 6d in the pound for a shop sale, 1/- in the pound from any sales to customers he called on, and, if he introduced a customer personally, he received 2/- in the pound.

Jimmy was now so much a part of the Denham family that when they moved from Princes Street to 150 Hilltown, he went with them. There his at-home playing was restricted to the kitchen as there was not the same set up of pletties. Mrs Pullar lived in the flat below and often told Mrs Denham how much she enjoyed Jimmy's music, but one day she said, 'But I canna say I care that much for yon drum!' Mrs Denham was puzzled, as there was only Jimmy and his accordion, but no drum. Suddenly she had a thought – it was his timekeeping foot. She made sure he had a cushion to mark time on after that!

Many types of people visited Forbes' shop at various times. One such person was Tom Walker, who worked as a sales representative for the G. Murdoch Trading Company of Glasgow. He heard Jimmy playing in the shop and was so impressed that he arranged for an offer to be made on behalf of Beltona Records. Beltona, who were making a name for themselves in the country, produced records at 1/6d each. Jimmy agreed to record with them using the 'L'Organola.'

Another visitor to the shop was a young man called Sandy Tulloch, who remembers the day and the events that led up to it:

I suppose I was about nine or ten when I first took a serious interest in Scottish country dance music. The Scout and Guide movement was vigorous in Montrose in the 1920s and we had regular country dances in the Black Watch drill hall in Mill Street. Strangely enough, my earliest recollection of a catchy tune was the *Morpeth Rant* – not really a Scottish tune at all but good to dance to and full of rhythm. At that time I played the moothie and was beginning to understand the workings of a mandolin. I was able to play some of the commoner traditional tunes, and at one of the concerts in St John's Church hall, I was asked to accompany Jim McHardie from Usan, who played an International Melodeon. I remember it well. Absolutely rectangular with sharp corners bound in nickel-plated brass work. The palettes were on the outside for all to see. Two stops – I suppose the precursors of treble couplers – were sticking out like organ stops on top and there were four incredible bass clappers which never seemed to harmonise with the treble, but acted in a way like bagpipe drones. Also a 'breather', which took in great gasps of air or exhaled equally noisily when a difficult passage had to be played. Jim McHardie's box was a two-row and with this arrangement it was possible to play in C or B, or perhaps D, G and A, but the flats were difficult, if not impossible. I was greatly taken with this instrument and decided there and then that this was to be it. The mandolin was not exactly forgotten but, from then on, took second place.

My Scout Master, Mr Potter, was good enough to give me a very simple instrument – only a single row treble and two bass notes – but I practised away until I had managed to master the bellows work to a certain extent. Having played the mouth organ, the principle came fairly naturally to me. Each button is responsible for two notes, a half tone in between, one with a press action of the bellows, one on the draw. The scale of C for instance would press, draw, press, draw, press draw, draw press. The bass accompaniment, such as it was, had to synchronise with the bellows action. The simple chords appeared to please everybody at the time but are sheer torture to listen to nowadays. I practised away at country dance tunes and gradually increased my repertoire as far as this very simple instrument would allow.

I collected records of the great Peter Wyper and played them over and over on an ancient gramophone with a huge sounding horn – just like the one with the faithful dog on the HMV records. I think it was about 1934/1935 that I was down at the fair ground in Montrose and I heard a melodeon recording on a gramophone at one of the stalls. I had thought Peter Wyper brilliant but this record surpassed anything I had ever heard before. I hung around and asked questions. The record was a Regal–Zonophone and the player was one James Shand. For me this was it – I became a Jimmy Shand fan there and then.

I practised on my single row box until frustration set in. I just didn't have the range of notes required. At that time,

J.T. Forbes of Dundee advertised an instrument called the Double Ray British Chromatic Accordion. There were two models – the Standard, away beyond my pocket money range and the De Luxe, far beyond my wildest dreams at £8 10s.! A glimmer of hope arose when an aunt of mine announced that she had a piano she did not want and that if I could do a deal with Forbes, I could have it for the asking. I saved up the 3/4d required for a return ticket to Dundee, found my way up from the Tay Bridge station to the shop and the deal was completed. They would collect the piano from Montrose and I would go away the proud owner of a Double Ray De Luxe complete with case, and a 'tutor' by Charles S. Forbes and James Shand.

Jimmy's picture, even in those days, showed a balding top, and in all the days I have known him, he hasn't changed a bit. Mr Forbes assured me that the reeds in this accordion would ring out loud and clear about the sound of a full orchestra. He would get his demonstrator to give me a tune, and sure enough the object of my hero-worship appeared, and with no obvious bellows movement, and fingers that seemed to flow without hand movement, I had my first experience of hearing Jimmy Shand 'live'. I suppose this was around 1934/35. I often wonder if Jimmy spotted an enthusiast at the time, but although it was a year or two later before I got to know him well, I think the beginnings of a lifetime friendship started there and then.

Once the Beltona contract got underway, the company advertised Jimmy as 'James Shand' and promoted him as one of their stars. Among the other musicians on their books were bothy ballad singer Willie Kemp (who also played the Jew's harp, ocarina and tin whistle), Curly McKay (another accordionist), and Donald Davidson, a master on the mouth organ.

Since his move to Dundee, the Denhams had always assured Jimmy that his family and friends would always be welcome. Jimmy knew this was true and one day he brought in a new friend, a pretty young waitress who worked at the Station Hotel in Leven. Her name was Anne Anderson and she knew Jimmy through one of her brothers who was interested in motorbikes. Anne also knew Nancy Brand, Jimmy's sister, who lived in Leven. Jimmy transported Anne between Leven and Dundee on a succession of motorbikes which they also used to visit relatives or go on sight-seeing trips.

'He was quite likely to set out on a Norton and come back on a New Imperial,' said George Denham. 'Terrible lad for swapping and doing deals!'

Anne and Jimmy decided to get married after Mr Anderson died, and set a date for the following January. The Forbes' shop lassies decided that Jimmy would not escape the time-honoured custom of every groom-to-be, and decorated him with coloured crepe paper and confetti the night before the wedding. They then led him through the streets to his lodgings, shouting and singing, making him carry a chamber pot filled with salt with a carrot stuck into it.

Jimmy and Anne's wedding

The next day, 24 January 1936, the roads in Fife were very icy and Jimmy and his family guests were half an hour late arriving at Colinsburgh Town Hall from East Wemyss. Fortunately the hall keeper had allowed access to the drink supply, so the Andersons did not notice the delay too much. After the wedding the newlyweds had a meal in the upstairs café in Edinburgh's Woolworths, as they had to wait for a train to take them to Peebles. Their honeymoon was spent at the house of Mr and Mrs John Maul, a couple Jimmy had met some time before on one of his demonstration tours of the Scottish Borders.

Jimmy and Anne found that they had little difficulty in getting a house, and when they returned to Dundee they moved into 95 Ellengowan Drive to set up their home. Jimmy's Aunt Rachel, who had become the Shand housekeeper after his mother died and sister Nancy married, was very generous in helping to furnish the new home.

Another highlight in the Shands' year was that Jimmy managed to buy his first car, a second-hand Morris 8, which cost £32 10s.

The following year, 1937, saw the birth of their first son Erskine James Shand on 1 March, while the widely promoted Beltona records by James Shand went up in price from 1/6d to 2s. An advertisement in the *People's Journal* stated they were now by 'Jimmy Shand of Dundee'. In the 7 August issue, an article about Jimmy, accompanied by a small photograph, appeared in the same newspaper. It said:

> Dundee has produced many musicians of note. Mr James Shand took his position in the list of those who have made good in this sphere when he made his debut over the air on Thursday night by giving a solo performance on the accordion.
>
> Mr Shand is well fitted for his task. Champion Button Key Accordionist of Scotland, he has been playing the instrument since he was six years old, 22 years ago, and is well known all over Scotland. He is accordion demonstrator with J.T. Forbes, Music Seller, Dundee and a star recordist of accordion music. He has little time for jazz and prefers the

spirited national music of Scotland, Ireland and the
Continent... Goes as far as the borders, plays at concerts,
dances and garden fêtes, and has appeared locally at the
Victoria and Plaza at charity performances.

The title 'Champion Button Key Accordionist of Scotland' was
not something that Jimmy had been awarded or one that he
claimed. Beltona just decided to call him that in the
promotional material they distributed.

In October 1937, Charles Forbes recruited to his staff a piano
accordionist called Louis Cabrelli. An audition over the
telephone impressed Forbes and a Glasgow record company,
an arrangement was made and a deal completed. Another
Forbes idea was to call in a film advertising unit and film
Jimmy playing *The Marquis of Huntly's Farewell*. Playing the
most intricate passage Jimmy's fingers seemed almost like a
blur on the screen. The film was shot on silent stock and when
Jimmy went along to the Victoria Theatre in Dundee to see it,
one of his records was played to accompany it. The fast moving
fingers were seen on the screen all right but the tune chosen,
The Bonnie Lass o Bon Accord, was far too slow.

Louis Cabrelli joined Jimmy as a demonstrator and when
they toured the country with Charles Forbes, both types of
accordion were expertly promoted. It did happen every now
and then that a customer, mesmerised with what they had seen
and heard, would take on something beyond their paying and
playing ability. There was one young farm lad that Jimmy
remembers well. The boy had visited the Forbes stand at the
Angus Show in Brechin, put down a payment on a Black Dot
Double Ray box and proudly taken it home. He paid a few
instalments and then the payments stopped. For a while he
could not be traced and then Forbes heard he was working on a
farm near Carnoustie and Jimmy was asked to go and see him:

He had had an injury at his work and there was nae
National Health at that time and the laddie had just got
intae difficulties and he couldna pay his account, so I was
asked to visit him this night and I mind it was a lovely nicht.

I'd been at Aberdeen as a matter o fact, coming in fae Aberdeen comin doon inta Carnoustie. I comes inta the ferm – knocks on the bothy door and asked if the young lad was in. Aye. Then he comes oot. Aye, and he hudna seen a razor for aboot twa months, I think, and he was red heeded and he had red stubble – just a young lad, ye ken. I says 'Hello Andy,' and he says 'Aye.'

I says 'You ken me,' and he said 'Aye, you're Shand.'

I says 'You'll ken why I'm here son?'

'Aye, you'll be here for the box.'

'Aye, but,' I says, 'I would rather that you could pay the box and keep it,' – cause he had paid quite a bit.

'Nae, I canny afford it,' he says, 'you'll just need to tak it awa. Play me a tune afore ye go.'

So I didna want to attract too much attention – summer's nicht, and there was hooses roon aboot. Soon as the melodeon started to play the doors were opening again and I got kind o embarrassed because I was gonna tak his box. However, I played twa or three tunes and he says to me, 'Play *Dovecot Park*,' so I played *Dovecot Park* and I says 'I'll hae to go noo Andy.'

'Aye,' he says, 'gies a shot afore ye tak it awa,' and he taks it. He sat doon on the bothy winda and when he started to play – well, started to draw oot and in – oh! it was like nothing on earth, nothing, so I says 'What was that, Andrew?' He says 'That was *Dovecot Park*.'

I didna like to say it wisna, but he says 'You ken when you lads selt me this melodeon and in the book, the tutor, it says *Play at sight the very same night!* I've had it for twa years and I canny play it yet!'

Oh dear it was a laugh, it was true.

So much for a sales gimmick!

Four

Charles Forbes was nothing if not a sales promoter, and the following was a typical advert for reasonably-priced boxes.

Are You A Two-row Player?
Then let Jimmy Shand show you how much easier and better a three-row is to handle. His demonstration costs you nothing – but is worth a lot.

Here, or in the Perth branch, or in your own home; he visits
ALL DISTRICTS
Three-voice, Three-row Instruments (Shand keyboard)
from £7. 7s. 6d.

Forbes' musical knowledge was also very useful to Jimmy in his early days of writing tunes. Jimmy recalls, 'The first tune I wrote was *Lunan Bay*. In fact I didna write it – it was Forbes that wrote it doon on music for me.' Jimmy diddled and Forbes listened. When asked why he had called it *Lunan Bay*, he replied, 'Well, funny enough, I was going to Aberdeen to hear Harry Gordon. I was on the motorbike and went up through Dundee and Arbroath, Montrose and I aye mind o passin this sign "Lunan Bay 2 miles" and I'd never seen Lunan Bay, and for many years efter.' The finished waltz tune quickly entered the Scots country dance repertoire.

1938 was to be another year in which the fortunes of Jimmy, Anne and their baby son improved, although the doting parents were worried about the persistent dampness in the house which they could not get rid of despite many efforts.

A picture of Jimmy and Louis Cabrelli appeared in an issue of the *People's Journal* in October 1938. The newspaper also contained a story about how they had been chosen as the two most outstanding accordion players in Britain. One of the benefits from these honours was an invitation to play at the annual Accordion Day Festival in London before 1,000 other accordionists the following month. The Accordion Festival was a wonderful success for both of them and it is safe to say Charles Forbes was quite pleased as well.

Jimmy was also going from strength to strength as a recording star, with more than a dozen successful records in circulation. Whenever the record-buying public thought of the button-key accordion they thought of Jimmy Shand, and vice versa. Jimmy had come a long way from being a navvy, less than five years before. He was now a white collar worker and his hands were now used to steering motor vehicles and creating musical tunes from a combination of reeds, bellows and buttons. He still retained his interest in working with wood by making model boats for the Denham boys and Jimmy junior.

Jimmy and Anne decided they were going to move to a better house, but finding a good rented house was not as easy as they had hoped. Most young newlyweds had to move from one set of furnished rooms to another before they managed to rent a house of their own. Anne and Jimmy had been lucky when they set up home by moving into rented accommodation right away. Now they wanted to rent a better house they found it was not so easy. They had to become involved in the dreary round of knocking on the office doors of house factors, enquiring if they had anything on their books and being cut off in mid sentence by frosty-faced clerks. There was the advertising, the answering of adverts and the mad dashing around to follow up rumours of possible exchanges, and at the end of the day still not having a house key.

Dundee Corporation were building houses but at a rate which was making little impact on the city's huge problems of insanitary vermin-infested slums and chronic overcrowding. It was not unusual for families to have to wait twenty years or more on a waiting list for a new house. There was one solution which was quite a thought for somebody of Jimmy's background – *buy* a house!

Many things were considered by Anne and Jimmy before they reached a decision. Were they trying to be above themselves? Would there be a regular supply of paying playing engagements? After all, hadn't paying up a box at five bob a week been less than easy at one time? How much would it cost? Would they get a mortgage? It may seem strange that they were so cautious, but they were both brought up never to take anything for granted.

When they decided to purchase, they followed the path of many people at that time and bought it through the Co-operative Building Society. For a deposit of £37 they moved into their own house at 16 Sutherland Street, in a quiet cul-de-sac just across from a public park. The view from the back of the house stretched over the old tenements, little shops and narrow streets, the chimneys and spires of Lochee on to a wonderful panorama of the Sidlaw hills.

The house itself was a brand new, semi-detached, villa consisting of a living room, two bedrooms, a kitchenette and a bathroom. The mortgage was less than £3 per month and the cash price £545. Jimmy's wages were £3 a week plus varying amounts of commission.

Jimmy was never content with his performances and was always striving to do something to improve the instruments he used. He went back to Charles Forbes and explained what he wanted and again a new specification including a completely new chart of the keyboard was prepared. The new accordion required 40 treble, 105 bass and 4 sets of reeds and was to be finished in real Pearloid with 'Shand' in brilliants. The details were promptly sent to Hohner in Germany.

Accordion sales were increasing all the time, and one of the reasons for this was undoubtedly the touring demonstrations Jimmy took part in with Charles Forbes and Louis Cabrelli. The more sales they made the more commission they earned: thus everyone was happy. They continued their policy of visiting all parts of Scotland, and one area which was particularly receptive was the east coast. Here they played to groups of mill hands, miners, farm lads and fishermen, who traditionally always had a box or fiddle to express their melancholia and to squeeze out the hornpipes, reels and schottisches as well as vamp when accompanying the singers.

Dundee was thought to have more box players per head of population than any other city in Britain. In 1938, over seventy players from Dundee entered for the British College of Accordionists' examination and new clubs were being formed throughout the district.

For a number of years Jimmy had been considered a master musician and celebrity by his fellow players but his fame was quickly spreading to the general public. Like 'Hoover' for vacuum cleaners and 'Singer' for sewing machines, whenever people talked about accordionists or accordions, the name 'Shand' would inevitably come up.

Another person who was widely recognised by accordionists was of course Louis Cabrelli. He was a prodigy in his own right: by the age of ten he was playing an International button-key box. When his father brought him a piano key instrument from Italy he changed over. He had to teach himself to play by listening to the records of Pietro and Guido Diero for hours on end, as there were so few similar instruments in Scotland. Talent scouts for the *Casey's Court* revue, which was appearing at Dundee's Victoria Theatre, heard him play, signed him up and introduced him to show business. For a while he had a marvellous time for a young laddie. He was delighting audiences with his virtuosity on the piano-accordion, and he was being paid. Eventually the lifestyle wore him down – moving all over Britain, from one set of theatrical digs to another, playing exactly the same tunes night after night, never having time to relax – enough was enough. He did not want to continue on the showbusiness treadmill. He needed time to study and wanted to go on improving, so he gave up performing to enable him to *play* more. As part of his musical development he had dealings with Hohner, and in conjunction with their Italian designer, Morino, a box referred to as the *Louis* Morino was made in 1937. Then he was ready to be 'discovered' again by Charles Forbes. Jimmy uses two words to describe Louis Cabrelli, 'a genius': exactly the same words Louis used to describe Jimmy.

By June 1939 Jimmy had received his new accordion from Germany and he was very pleased, as it proved to be a first-class instrument. This really was the prototype of what was to become known as the celebrated Hohner 'Shand Morino'.

Sandy Tulloch, a regular visitor to the Shands' home, recalls:

In 1936 I went to University College Dundee Medical School and was always being asked to play at Smokers and other functions in the Union. The faithful Double Ray was in great demand and I must have been a trial and tribulation to the long suffering 'bunk wives', as our landladies were called in those days. I used to go out fairly regularly to the Diddling Competitions which were held in the country districts at that time. They were great fun. Later, when I rose to the dizzy heights of a three-row box, I was disqualified – the competition was strictly for two-row melodeons.

I think I next saw Jimmy at such a concert in Coupar Angus. I remember vividly a competitor for the mouth organ getting through the first eight bars of the *Mason's Apron* then he stopped, took out his teeth and put them on top of the piano, announcing that he 'couldna play nane wi thae bluidy falsers in.' Then a march, strathspey and reel from a shy Jimmy Shand, who could hardly be persuaded to come out from behind a draught screen on the small stage. But shy or not, the magic was there and this time Jimmy had a magnificent box, a three-row Hohner Special with full bass accompaniment on the left hand. This was something only found on piano and continental accordions and was a revelation to me. I found out later that this was the first in a line of Hohner Specials built for Jimmy in collaboration with their head designer, Morino.

I'll never forget that accordion. It was away in front of its time in design, range and tone. I've never played an instrument that handled as easily as that one. The reeds were hand made, specially long in the tongue and answered instantly to the slightest pressure or change of bellows movement. It was a four voice accordion with a coupler to bring in the lower octave reeds. The bass side was superb and had full chording. The button action was unique – three row of buttons linked to two rows of palettes in some miraculous fashion. The keyboard was real mother of pearl, the buttons very nearly flush and so firm and positive in action that staccato triplets were a joy to play, something at that time distinctive to button box playing. Since then piano accordions have improved beyond all recognition but at that time, for staccato playing, nothing could touch the button box, especially when played by Jimmy Shand.

My Double Ray De Luxe now looked a poor toy compared to this magnificent instrument. I started saving and by 1939 had the necessary £40 to buy a three-row Scandalli with eighty bass arrangement. It was, of course, the British Chromatic System. With Jimmy's guidance I made some modifications. First, the air intake had to be almost blocked off with sticky paper so that I didn't 'gasp' the accordion when playing. Then the composition buttons were replaced with real, smooth, mother of pearl buttons supplied by my favourite nurse at Maryfield, who was to become my wife in 1942.

Jimmy had a workshop in a garret above Watt's in the Wellgate, Dundee. Later on I learned a great deal from Tommy Burns, but at that time we sat in Sutherland Street with a used razor blade and a set of needle files making sure that every reed was in perfect tune and every 'leather' in prime condition. I used to go to Sutherland Street about once a week for lessons – how Anne put up with me I'll never know. And poor Jimmy – he must have tholed an awful lot as I struggled my way through the various exercises in three-row technique. The British Chromatic is a complicated instrument.

Looking back, it would have been much simpler to use the Continental Chromatic but my heart was always set on the traditional melodeon system. It seemed to me to be essentially Scottish and the right instrument for playing Country Dance music. Each button plays two notes as in a melodeon. Each octave is entirely different from the one above or the one below and gets more complex as you go on. For instance, in the higher registers a mental somersault is required. A note of higher pitch may have to be played on a lower button. In the lower registers the opposite holds good. A curious and desperately complicated system. With three rows there are a certain number of duplicates – notes that can be played on the 'press' or on the 'draw' of the bellows. Left hand action is all important and the use of these alternative fingering systems is the secret of smooth playing and 'phasing' the music. If I could justify the expenditure, I would order yet another 'Special' with four rows of treble keys and perhaps a row of minor thirds on the bass side, but at today's prices this dream will never be realised.

I remember my first exercise set by Jimmy. The six measures of the 6/8 march, *The Atholl Highlanders*. It was here that Jimmy showed me some of the secrets of crisp, smooth fingering and bellows work. Later we went on to the 2/4 marches such as the *Balkan Hills* and *John MacDonald of Glencoe*. Jimmy was a tremendous help and inspiration at this time. The house at Sutherland Street was a home from home, not only for myself, but for a great number of other enthusiasts and musicians. I never saw the living room empty or the table cleared. Poor Anne – she seemed to have half the musical population of Dundee and district to feed and look after. They were the most generous and kindest folk I have ever known.

As his fame became more widespread, Jimmy was asked to play in different parts of the country and he was delighted to travel to the different venues in his first *new* car, an 8 hp. Ford.

From late in his teens Jimmy had begun to develop a *wide* parting in his hair and he tried many things to encourage new growth on his scalp. For a period of time no treatment or lotion was too bizarre to be tried or tested. There was, however, one particular prescription which cost nothing and anyone could try if they were getting thin on top – stewed grass! Unfortunately, it did not work for Jimmy but maybe he did not try it early enough, or he may have been a particularly difficult case, or maybe he did not keep applying the treatment long enough or... What was this wonderful treatment? Not a potion, but a lotion, applied to the appropriate part of the head as a poultice. Mrs Denham had first brewed up the concoction in her kitchen when Jimmy first came to live with her in 1933.

Jimmy learned to accept that his baldness was really his brains growing through! He remembers an incident when he was playing in the Victoria Hall in Coupar Angus. The hall was packed full but outside one latecomer successfully pleaded to be allowed in to see the great Jimmy Shand. Once inside his astonished reaction was heard throughout the hall: 'Christ! He's nae bluidy chicken, is he?'

In the late 1930s, Wull Kydd went to see Jimmy about buying a Borzoni accordion – he was quite convinced that it was the box for him – but, after listening to Jimmy explain that his personal experience of the instrument was that he had difficulty in 'gettin wind intae the inner ra', Wull changed his mind and bought a Scandalli instead. 'Och, but he did hae a Borzoni later on when done!' Jimmy recalls. Around that time, Wull also introduced Jimmy to left-handed fiddler and lorry driver, Dave Ireland. Dave, like Jimmy, was virtually self-taught in his instrument: he had picked up the bowing and fingering on his family's fiddle, although later he got a few lessons from Jim Barrie of Broughty Ferry. Jimmy and Dave played together sporadically over the years, but constantly kept in touch.

More of Jimmy's recordings were issued onto the market, Beltona promoting them with the heading 'By Shand'. They emphasised their distribution by saying, 'These Are The Newest and they include *Rocky Mountain Medley; She'll Be Comin' Round The Mountain, Can I Sleep In Your Barn? Hand Me Down My Walking Cane, Chicken Reel, Turkey In The Straw,* and a *Blue Ridge Medley – De Ole Banjo, Kingdom Comin, Oh Susannah!*'

Another record provided music for a *Soft Shoe Dance; Lily of Laguna,* and *Shine On Harvest Moon,* backed by *The Noble Duke of York,* and *Tavern In The Town.* There was nothing there to put a wiggle in a kilt... but one side did offer *Stonehaven March* and *Scotland The Brave.*

Of course, plenty of recordings of reels, strathspeys and schottisches were to follow and within a few months *Another Grand Selection By The Champion Performer On The Button-key Accordion* appeared.

Illness is no respector of fame and at this time the Shands needed the services of one Dr Jameson who was at King's Cross Hospital, Dundee, when Anne was admitted suffering from diphtheria. He writes:

Three days later, their 2 years and 6 months son Erskine was also admitted with the same disease. Jimmy himself, as a contact, had a throat swab taken but this proved negative, so that he was left to fend for himself at home and was able to visit the hospital regularly to see his family. Both Mrs Shand and Erskine made good recoveries without developing any complications, and were allowed home after spending 4–6 weeks in hospital.

It transpired that Dr Jameson was a talented ukulele player: he used to accompany himself in full-blooded renderings of bothy ballads and other songs. He quickly became a firm friend of the family.

With tension growing in Europe, the local authorities in Scotland slowly began to make preparations for the possibility of air attacks. Some were convinced it would never happen, but Dundee had been voicing concern for a while. On 10 July 1937, a Dr R.C. Buist spoke to the St Andrew's Ambulance Association and commended the suitability of the old railway tunnel which ran through a shoulder of The Law, the 500 foot hill that rises above Dundee, as an air raid shelter. In October 1938 a 'spokesman' was quoted in the newspaper as saying that the same tunnel could hold six to seven thousand people easily if needed.

One person who had first hand experience of what was going on in Europe was Louis Cabrelli, as he had been in the habit of making regular visits there: as a representative of Hohner, he particularly made many appearances in Germany. A piece of advice he had been given before going there was 'Don't play any Jewish music.' This meant he had to change his normal repertoire, as he usually enjoyed playing some of the works of Mendelssohn and Gershwin. He also found that British music was not very popular either; although on one occasion, when he was asked to play in a large underground hall to an audience of more liberal-minded Germans, anything he played from *Rhapsody in Blue* to *Lambeth Walk* was greeted with loud applause. Whenever he was shown round a factory he noticed the walls were covered by large posters of Hitler.

One day he turned to Willie Black, the representative of a Dundee firm of music sellers and remarked that the penetrating eyes seemed to follow them wherever they went. He then turned and made a face at one of the posters – somebody noticed this, reported him and the next day he was warned about his conduct.

A month or so before war was declared, the music trade became aware that, although accordions were still popular, the market was becoming saturated. The likelihood of being able to import any instruments would soon be impossible and many potential buyers were already signing up for the armed forces.

Although he enjoyed travelling all over Scotland playing and demonstrating, Jimmy was often away from home which he disliked intensely. After Anne and his son got back to full fitness, Jimmy looked around for some other kind of employment. He took a job driving a furniture van for Robertson of Barrack Street, Dundee, leaving Forbes on the best of terms. When war was declared, there was only one thing the speed-mad enthusiast wanted to do and that was volunteer to fly with the RAF. However, his unreliable digestive system – which

Fireman Jim

Jimmy was convinced was a legacy of his block-making days – put paid to any service in the armed services. One organisation which was delighted to have him, though, was the Fire Service, and between his hours of duty he could still play to his ain folk.

Since the mid-thirties Jimmy had been making regular radio broadcasts as a solo accordionist, and this routine was not disturbed by the advent of war. His lively and cheerful music was like a tonic to the listeners, in contrast to the sometimes depressing news about the early fighting. He was, of course, already a legend to his fellow box players, piano players, fiddlers and other musicians who had a deep love of Scottish traditional airs, to say nothing of the growing band of enthusiasts for national folk music: say the name 'Shand' in farm kitchens, bothies and mining communities and a smile would greet you and feet would begin to tap.

Those who had Beltona records handled them with great care, listened to them for hours attentively and were very loathe to loan them to anyone. Wireless sets were carefully checked to ensure there was no discharge of the wet accumulator or that the dry battery had not gone flat. Those who did not have a wireless or others whose sets were not working made arrangements in advance with friends for 'a listen'. Nobody wanted to take the chance of missing Jimmy on the wireless, and folk would hurry home to tune in at the right time.

For those in and around Dundee, the hustle and bustle of the times seemed to involve everyone. There were busy war work schemes operating round the clock, as well as Home Guard duties and fire watching rotas. The Fire Brigade was constantly rehearsing and drilling when not attending actual fires and everybody put in that little extra effort. Whenever dances were held they were attended with enthusiasm and regarded as a relief from austere conditions. Jimmy played regularly, fire duties permitting, at many of the venues and always received a great reception, but surprising though it may seem, he regarded this period in his career as the time *he began to learn to play!* He explains: 'What I mean is this. Although I'd been playing Scots dances lang enough, it wasna *disciplined* playin. Ye see, there had been nae set length for a dance. Ye played until the dancers began tae get tired, but a' Scots country dances have a set length – sae many bars tae each figure. This I learned fae Doug Henderson at the Empress first of a', and later at the instructional dances at Rockwell School. I'm no kiddin ye, for the first time I was learnin tae play Scots music richt!'

Five

Jimmy was not being modest when he said he was learning to play, he meant it. The Dockland Ballroom, the Empress, under the very efficient management of the popular Mrs Duncan, had established a regular routine of Old Time Nights. Jimmy was introduced to these initially in 1938 by Doug Henderson who had been teaching dancing for some years. Doug instructed in Scottish Country Dancing for an hour before the Old Time sessions started, and he asked Jimmy to play for the lessons rather than use the resident band. Doug regarded Jimmy as being better than the band, while Jimmy learned a great deal from Doug.

Few people, if any, could teach Jimmy anything about *playing* Scots music; what he learned from these Empress sessions was *how long* to play. Doug helped him understand the all important relationship between a particular dance and something like four by thirty-two bars. All dances have their prescribed procession of steps, their ordered lengths and this *timely* information was eagerly absorbed and filed away in Jimmy's wonderful musical memory.

On one occasion Jimmy was asked to recommend a really professional Scottish Country Dance Band for an ambitious Scottish evening. The chosen band travelled through from the west but the evening was a shambles. For most of the dances they were still playing after the dancers had completed their sets. At other times they finished too early, leaving the dancers swishing around, their sandalled feet thumping on the floor. By the end of the evening it became obvious that if Jimmy could provide his own band for the next big Scottish event he could name his own fee.

Not long afterwards Jimmy led his own band, playing for Scottish country dancing on a Monday night in St Patrick's Hall in Maitland Street, Dundee, run by Craigie Football Club. The band members, like Jimmy, all had their own daytime jobs, so their playing was on a strictly part-time basis. There was always the possibility that, because of the war situation, they could not always guarantee they would be free to play. Among the early band members was Jim Cameron, a lemonade man from Kirriemuir, who played the fiddle, and his accordion-playing daughter, Mae. The others were Dave Donaldson and Allen Reid. The great enthusiasm for spirited music and dancing meant Jimmy and his band had as much work in 1940 as they could sensibly take.

Early in 1941 a severe 'flu epidemic left Jimmy on the search for a replacement drummer. A friend of Jimmy's, Jerry McCafferty, learned about the vacancy in the dunt section when he spoke to Jimmy in the Fire Station. Jerry's advice was instantaneous: 'So ye need a drummer? Cheer up – that's nae bother! Wee Owney McCabe – he's yer man! Ye'll get him at the sawmill in Lochee.'

Jimmy went along to the sawmill and asked for the recommended drummer. He was taken by surprise when Owen McCabe appeared, hardly higher than Jimmy's bottom jacket button. Recovering his voice Jimmy said, 'Want a job the

(l-r): Jimmy Shand, Willie Ogilvie, Mae Cameron, Jim Cameron

nicht? I've a band playing at Alyth an we're needin a drummer.' Apparently Owen was delighted to be asked and excitedly told his wife when he got home that he had a drumming job with a chap called Shand, whom he had never seen before, but the extra few bob would come in handy. On the way to Alyth, Owen was very nervous; however, by the time he got back home his confidence was completely shattered! When his wife asked how he had got on Owen confessed it had not gone well, as Jimmy had continually turned round and given him dirty looks. Fortunately, it was explained to Owen over the next few days that the constantly shy Jimmy had a habit of moving his head to the side whenever he felt the audience attacking him with their eyes – a habit that Owen had misinterpreted as Jimmy's disapproval. Much relieved on hearing this, Owen decided to stay with the band!

Dave Ireland, the left-handed fiddler, had his own band but he usually sat in with Jimmy at St Patrick's on a Monday night. George McKelvey, piano accordionist, played with Dave Ireland on Saturday nights in the village of Longforgan. One Monday he went with the fiddler to meet Jimmy and quickly accepted an invitation to become second box player in Jimmy's band.

George was another of those box players who had started with a melodeon whilst he was still at school. During the 1926 strike, a travelling miner musician had offered a piano accordion for sale. It was not a very common instrument in those days, but with the help of some sweepstake winnings and his mother's purse, George bought it. After practising whenever he had a spare moment, George eventually became part of a musical trio, playing at dances in small halls. As their reputation grew, they moved on to better halls and higher fees. The other two in the group were drummer Stuartie Foy, who would sometimes dress up in 'Dame' costume and deliver comic monologues, and Tommy McDaniel who often played the piano in the McKelvey house and was often asked to 'stay on' for his meals.

There were still some Dundee dance halls which were

considered oary (less than respectable) and one, because of its long narrow layout, was known as *The Palais de Loabby*. Working in some of these halls could endanger your instruments as well as your health; thankfully Jimmy never had to play in them!

Being asked to join a Shand band was an opportunity that George intended to make the most of, and did, for three weeks – until he was called up. Three months later he was back playing, having been invalided out of the forces because of stomach trouble.

The most regular band line-up at that time was Jimmy and George on accordions, Johnny Knight, piano, Dave Ireland, fiddle, and Owen McCabe on drums. Jimmy, by all accounts, had an easy-going rapport with his players which enabled them to appreciate and perform the extremely individual Shand selections and arrangements. Surely, the inimitable Shand Band 'sound' could only be achieved after many long sessions of rehearsal, playing and replaying, refining and polishing hour after hour? Not so, as Jimmy explained: 'We jist somehow seemed tae hit on a way o playin Scottish dance music that folk like.'

The first band members (l-r): George McKelvey, Dave Ireland,
Owney McCabe, Jimmy Shand, Johnny Knight

There were no flashy, fancy twiddly bits in the band music, the style was simple and clear. Sandy Tulloch recalls:

I was at Maryfield in Dundee as a clinical clerk by this time. Jimmy and the band played in St Patrick's Hall in Maitland Street every Monday night and I used to be allowed to sit in with them. There I got to know and make a lasting friendship with Dave Ireland, the left-handed fiddler. I played with George McKelvey, who played a Hohner accordion with a curved keyboard, which he changed later for a Morino model and which is still playing as well today as it was then. Also with Owen McCabe, the drummer – wonderful wee Owney, sadly missed now. I think the pianist was Willie Robb, but it is a long time ago now.

I used to sit in at the back but at times I was so intent on the fingering that I would miss the change of tune when the time came. Jimmy used to turn round with a wee smile and a shake of the head and I'd realise with a start that I was out on my own, and had to get back on the right tune as quick as I could, hoping that only the band had noticed. I soon realised that playing Scottish country dance music with Jimmy Shand was an exact science. Jimmy chose his tunes with care and gave each couple a change of tune and a change of key. It soon became second nature to know all the dances and to change automatically for an 8x32, 8x40 or 9x32 as the dance required. Jimmy had no use for so-called 'original' tunes if they were poor music and did not fit the dance. He used to get in trouble with the Scottish Country Dance Society and the BBC about this, and later in Glasgow I suffered the same way. But I agree entirely with him in this matter. What use is a 4/4 reel if it is virtually unplayable and unpleasant to the ear? And who decides what is the 'original' tune anyway? I'm sure Scott Skinner did not compose an 'original' tune for a dance that was invented long after his death!

It was about this time I was in the Odeon Cinema at Coldside when an accordion record was played during the interval. The music was new to me, a lively continental, but I was sure the style was Jimmy Shand's. I went to the Manager's office and got the details. It was Jimmy and he was playing a piece by Emile Vacher called *Triolets*. On the other side was a *Valse Musette*. As I got to know Jimmy better, whilst he was relaxed and off duty, I began to realise what an immense repertoire this man had – especially 'old time' music. He also played many continental numbers which I found very interesting and this interest has always remained with me. Curiously enough, although they sound complicated, I have always found them easier to play than a fast Scottish reel. These really sound out your technique on this type of accordion. These happy days at Sutherland Street and playing with Jimmy at every opportunity went on until 1942, when I got married and almost immediately left for medical service in the army. Needless to say, the box went with me and I continued to practice Scottish music and tried to improve my technique in continental-style playing.

During the war I listened to the continental accordion whenever I could and collected music in France, Belgium, Holland and Germany. I still have a large collection of this in my music cupboard. The Scandalli did well but, with only an 80 bass range, lacked the diminished seventh chords required in *Musette*, although never required in country dance music. Its use has gradually crept in but Jimmy considered it out of place in our type of music and said it was a chord to be used with care, and only when absolutely necessary. So I remained content with the accordion I had.

There were many restrictions and shortages during the war years which were borne with remarkable fortitude and prompted various types of improvisation. A booking was taken to play at a dance at Coupar Angus and a plan was devised to enable the band to get there and back despite petrol rationing. Each member of the band made their own way to Camperdown Gates – a large estate on the perimeter of Dundee – and a car took them to the dance. After many hours of playing to a very enthusiastic audience, they were driven back to the Gates and they then made their several ways home, in the blackout, carrying their instruments. Sometimes these late night walks would be through driving rain or snow.

Apart from a shortage of petrol, spare parts were not easy to come by and older cars tended to break down frequently. On one occasion, out of sheer desperation, a tyre was packed with grass but, like the hair-restoring poultice, it didn't do any good!

Another night the band arrived at Blairgowrie and found to their dismay that some of the drum kit had bounced its way off the top of the car. Despite this, Owney kept a precision beat all evening, with his side drums sitting on a chair.

A decision was soon taken that the band needed its own amplifying equipment and Owney was given the responsibility of providing it. Getting the heavy equipment and lugging it, with considerable difficulty, to their first booking was eventually achieved – only to be defeated in the end: the venue, Forteviot Hall, was lit by paraffin, not electricity! One person who was always pleased to see the band at Forteviot Hall was schoolboy Bill Powrie, as he was allowed to play his accordion for the company when the band had a tea interval. As the band left the platform he would always say, 'Tak yer time now lads!' His father, Will Powrie, was well known as a duettest and soloist on Beltona Records at a time when Jimmy was still awaiting his first contract. Bill Powrie's brother Ian, already a talented musician, was steadily building up his reputation as a fiddle player.

The increasingly enthusiastic receptions the band received made light of some of the difficulties they experienced through shortages or breakdowns. These were happy nights, with everyone going home in good spirits. One dark night after playing at Letham Hall, the band sped back to Dundee with Jimmy at the wheel of the car. Dave Ireland was sitting happily whistling a pipe tune, complete with grace notes, when the car hit a right angle bend. The car mounted the bank and it took all Jimmy's strength to wrestle it back down again on to the road. Dave was still whistling but as Jimmy said, 'That's a helluva long note, Dave!'

The war seemed to generate a greater enthusiasm for music, all kinds of music. Symphony concerts and ballet performances attracted large attendances in the evenings; while at lunchtimes it was standing room only in galleries, large and small halls, and even factory canteens, as various soloists gave classical recitals. Certainly, in many of the dance halls, the quicksteps and foxtrots were being challenged by the frantic extrovert gyrations of the jitterbug dancers – yet, this was the very time when the regular, precisely controlled measures of Scottish country dancing gracefully took over. In magnificent ballrooms resplendent with dazzling chandeliers and gilded cornices, kilted and sashed gentry gathered to dance the same patterns known to ladies and lairds for hundreds of years previously. Schoolrooms, barns, village halls and even tenement kitchens were commandeered and crowded with enthusiasts if there was need for a celebratory spree. Any excuse would do to break the dullness of war conditions – a joyful send off to newlyweds or the welcoming home on leave of a serviceman or woman. None of these happy occasions were ever complete without some old aunt (invariably called Jessie!), who could not sing to save herself, insisting on contributing a solo performance, much to everyone's amusement. These were the times to loosen the stays and take part in floor-dirling *hoochs* and birling rafter-rattling sessions accompanied by 'Tam' on the fiddle, 'Boab' on the box – or Jimmy Shand on records.

Whereas there had been few new dances for the past fifty years, the repertoire of Scottish country dances was now being quickly extended. Everybody had a great feeling of national pride and a more acute appreciation of their heritage. Musically speaking, the man who brought this into focus was Jimmy Shand.

Such was the popularity of Jimmy's regular solo radio broadcasts that he was asked to go to London to make a record in 1942. Jimmy remembers the reaction of Owney McCabe when he asked the drummer to go with him. 'London, Jim? *London*? Tae mak a record? Wait a minute – I – I'm no sure. I…' he stammered. 'Nothin tae worry about. Jist play as ye have been an we'll be a' richt,' Jimmy replied.

In London, their landlady told them about the air raid shelter in the basement of the house, and reminded them about the blackout regulations as they went upstairs, whilst Owney was already building up to a good worry about the following day's recording sessions! Jimmy had thrown back the curtains and opened the windows before they started to get into their

61

pyjamas, when the siren sounded. Jimmy quickly cautioned, 'Dinna switch the licht on!' There followed a pantomime of confusion as both of them banged into the walls, the furniture and each other, performing an absurd reel in the darkness striving to achieve the dignity of putting their trousers on. Such pleasantries as, 'Hell, nae wonder Owney – these are *yours!* – gies mine!' were exchanged. They finally were presentable enough to rush down to the basement, which they reached just in time for the 'All Clear' sound. The fact that the Luftwaffe decided to leave Owney undisturbed for the rest of the night meant he could fret about the different rhythms of jig, hornpipe, strathspey and reel and wonder if he had ever understood their different beats. One record was bad enough – but they were going to make six.

Next day in the recording studio, Jimmy and George Scott Wood, the studio pianist, patiently encouraged the small drummer, and eventually everything went well. When the recordings were issued, Beltona included in the advert in the Dundee newspapers, *featuring Owen McCabe, drums*. Although he went back to his day job of cutting less glamorous discs of wood for bobbins at the sawmill, Owney's thoughts were on the possibility that the future might offer a different and more creative way for him to earn his living.

Considering his family background and the fact that so many musicians were always in and around the house, it was inevitable that Erskine would be sent for music lessons. He was six in 1943 when he went to Miss Brown, a piano teacher. After a while Jimmy enquired how Erskine was getting on, as he seemed to spend a great deal of time rushing about in Lochee Park and had to be hauled in for his piano practice. Miss Brown assured Jimmy that his son was learning to play very well, 'but he just can't be bothered with the *music*,' she said. 'He picks up and plays the exercises 'by ear' all the time.' 'Mmm... Well, that'll no dae, will it?' said Jimmy, the very man who, until then had never played any other way! 'What d'ye think then?' he enquired. 'Suppose you bring him back when he's about eight,' was the reply.

The fame of the Shand Band was such that its name on a poster for a dance would guarantee a packed house. More and more people checked their radio listings to ensure they did not miss one of Jimmy's solo broadcasts and his charity work was greatly appreciated. His records were selling well, yet at times he was frustrated and depressed when he thought of how he had failed to get into the RAF, and had been prevented from playing an active part in the war. Normally temperate with alcohol, Jimmy began to indulge on occasion. He does not care to dwell on this period of his life except to say, 'Jist let's say that I maybe took a drap mair than usual at times, but pulled up afore I went aff the rails.'

Late in December 1944, Howard M. Lockhart, a producer and presenter with the BBC, telephoned and asked Jimmy if he could go through and play a selection of tunes on a programme on New Year's Day 1945. Jimmy remembers, 'I suggested tae him then, I says, "Would ye no prefer to hear a wee band instead o me masel," because it was easier playin wi the band. So he said to bring them through and I tell you it's quite true and frank, I took them through – we played and did the job and we never looked back since, and I was lucky because they a' blended fine – they maybe wurna perfect, but they were passable.'

Johnny Knight, who played the piano with the band, said shortly afterwards, 'The first broadcast from Glasgow on New Year's Day 1945 in Scottish Half Hour... That's what made the band, after that we *knew* we were a good band. I remember it well. There was an extra three minutes to play and we gave them *Scottish Reform*... "The finest playing of Scottish country dance music I've heard for a long while," said the producer. "You'll be hearing more from us!" we said, and within a month we were broadcasting from Aberdeen and Edinburgh.'

When the war ended there was a long series of welcome home concerts to add to the band's very busy schedule. Jimmy was released from the Fire Service before VE Day and obtained a job with a lorry contractor. He thought that his experiences of casual employment in the twenties and thirties would not be repeated, particularly in a period of chronic manpower shortage. He was wrong – he had the job for *one week*. He was in charge of the company's transport depot taking any orders over the phone. The problem was, the phone never stopped ringing and most of the callers wanted to speak to Jimmy rather than book lorries. Despite the fact they were all incoming calls, Jimmy was accused of using the phone for private purposes. His pithy reply was not necessarily musical, but would have had his old mining and navvying pals' heads nodding. He left and his next job with Tay Motor Lorries was a much longer and happier experience.

In mid August 1945, Jimmy and Anne (now pregnant with their second child) visited some of their relations in Fife. Driving from East Wemyss to Colinsburgh, they had just gone through Upper Largo when Jimmy felt pressurised by a covered army vehicle running too close behind. For the sake of his peace of mind he moved over to let it pass. A short time later he rounded Drumeldrie bend to find the van on its side and several Polish soldiers lying on the road. The van was a left-hand drive and the driver was wedged in his seat by an officer who had been thrown on top of him. Jimmy hauled the officer clear and freed the driver who was luckily unhurt, apart from a badly split nose. Anne, who was very upset by the incident, was left in the care of a woman from a nearby cottage and Jimmy drove the (still bleeding!) driver, a corporal, to the nearest doctor a mile away. The corporal ensured he did not sully the car's upholstery by having the presence of mind to use his beret to catch every drop! Anne was still recovering from the shock of the accident when, two weeks later, on 28 August, the Shands' second son, David Anderson Shand, was born. David was a Down's Syndrome baby and, like most parents in such a situation, Jimmy and Anne took a while to come to terms with this fact.

In musical terms the band had reached a high note. Every committee of every angling, bowls, curling, cycling, Darby and

Joan, football, golf, rugby, shinty, tennis and water polo club in Scotland seemed determined to book Shand's Band for their Grand Annual. This was to say nothing of the other associations, the Daughters of This, the Sons of That, the Guilds and the Fraternal Societies who also wanted them. Surely Jimmy was happy and contented with his undoubted success? No—! His response was to walk away, or rather drive, to Thurso, armed with plenty of petrol coupons, in the 1934 Austin 10 he had bought from Andrew Robertson, a local shore porter. Some speculated that the band's success had overwhelmed Jimmy and that the thought of standing in front of larger and larger crowds alarmed him. Others suggested he thought there was no future in Scottish dance music. However, Jimmy was quite clear in his mind as to what he was doing. 'Nae doot aboot still bein shy – an the bigger the croods the mair embarrassed I would get. As for there no bein a real future for my kind o music, well, maybe now that the war was oer, wi mair choice o entertainment, the Scottish country dancing boom would just fade awa,' he explained.

However, he didn't stay in Thurso; he went on to the Orkneys. Why? 'Well, I'd been there afore the war – played a few concerts, wi Jim Cameron an freens, that had been arranged by James W. Sinclair, a Kirkwall photographer. Fair fell in love wi the place. As a matter o fact, I caed my hoose in Sutherland Street "Malvern" efter his.'

What did Anne have to say about this move?

'Oh, we'd talked it over, of course. The idea was that I'd gae up there and get started selling musical instruments, and maybe a wee bit playing at niehts, then I'd bring up her and the bairns. Oh, I looked furrit tae it and Anne was agreeable.'

The sea journey to the islands was very rough and took almost double the normal sailing time. For days afterwards, Jimmy felt as if the ground was rocking. The wind blew, the rain lashed and the snow smothered Kirkwall for three months. During the day Jimmy worked in Sinclair's shop, venturing abroad at nights to play in concerts and at dances. Occasionally, getting to engagements meant embarking in tiny boats, hanging on to his box while they battled through mountainous waves and tides. One of the things that kept him going was the thought he was experiencing the worst of the weather during the winter and that things could only get better.

In the middle of January 1946, Jimmy planned a visit to Dundee. For several days before his flight it snowed and snowed and snowed. On the departure day, a raging gale seemed determined to break the restraining ropes and carry the little plane off on a crazy flight path. Standing in the rattling Nissen hut shelter which itself threatened to take off, Jimmy made a decision. If, and when, the plane made it back to the mainland, he would take up residence in Dundee again. He was not going to expose his wife and bairns to winters like the one he was experiencing. It was a stressful time for everybody on the bleak airfield. The potential passengers were assured that, yes, the plane would probably be going; all right, of course, it had gone in much worse weather – perhaps it may be just a wee bit late that was all and, och, there was nothing to worry about really…! Among the passengers was a young mother with her wee bairn, and the quiet composure she displayed helped to quell Jimmy's fears. It was a very bumpy, frightening flight and when at one time the mother was sick, Jimmy offered to nurse the bairn.

Jimmy was never as glad to see dry land as he was when the aeroplane landed at Aberdeen. The young mother and her child were taking another plane to London. 'A stout-herted bit o a lassie,' Jimmy thought to himself during his comfortable hour and a half train trip to Dundee!

Six

The news quickly got round Dundee that Jimmy was back, that he was back for good and that he was considering establishing a full-time band. Jimmy approached the obvious candidates to see if they were interested in joining his new venture. Owney got to Jimmy before he could seek him out! Dave Ireland was involved in a business venture and decided that full-time playing was not for him, so his place was taken by Angus Fitchet who had known Jimmy since the 1920s.

Angus had started playing the fiddle when he was very young, and by the time he was five years old he was helping to distribute music to cinema musicians who gathered in a hall in King's Road, Dundee, for practice sessions. Aged ten he played at dances, normally travelling to and from the venues sitting on the back of fiddler Jim Barrie's push-bike, hanging on to a couple of fiddles. Angus's father often cycled alongside carrying his own fiddle. By the time he was fourteen he had graduated to playing in cinemas, his fingering and bowing adapting quickly to catch the moods of the action on the silver screen. He got to know Jimmy through playing in the little music festivals which were held in the villages and small towns of Angus and Perthshire during the 1920s and '30s. Angus said, 'Jimmy could be called a breakthrough in box-playin. He was a revelation; naebody before had ever managed to get as much as he somehow could out of a melodeon.' One of the occasions Jimmy and Angus played together was in 1934 at the annual Charity concert for ex-ploughmen in Dundee's Foresters' Hall. Topping the bill was Sir Harry Lauder, Scotland's greatest star at the time.

Johnny Knight, who had taken over from Peggy Edwards in Jimmy's regular Maitland Street Hall engagements, was very happy to continue his contribution to the band as piano player, but he kept up his involvement in the printing trade.

George McKelvey worked in the calendar department at Baxter's Jute Mill. One evening, after completing a day's lapping (the final folding process after the starched and finished jute cloth had been pressed through hot rollers), George found Jimmy waiting for him at the mill gate. George despatched himself from Baxter's the following Friday.

The band was complete, and they were working full-time. What they did not realise was 'full-time' actually meant 'no limit on time'. Whereas before, engagements could only be fitted in after a day's work and could not be accepted very far from home, the potential venues were now all over Scotland and even beyond. If families had seen little of a musician father before, they would see even less of him now! This was not because the band relaxed in hotels before or after the more distant engagements; quite the opposite was the case. More often than not they would finish in the early hours of the morning at a venue down south and immediately pack their instruments and themselves into Jimmy's Morris car and head back home through the night to Dundee. If they were lucky they might snatch a few hours sleep before heading north to fulfil their next engagement. It was not unusual to be playing seven nights a week.

Jimmy would not have asked anybody to take the plunge into full-time playing if he had not organised a long list of pre-arranged engagements. How long was a long list? George McKelvey, who kept the diary, could point to the book and say, 'Jimmy used to give us the jobs for a year ahead at a time.'

There was South Shields one night, Glasgow the next. Playing Brampton on a Friday night and Aberdeen the next night did not leave much time for sleep. With more and more of the playing engagements in England the travelling increased. One evening they played in the Albert Hall in London, having performed in Inverness in Scotland the previous night.

There were other things which were beyond even the best laid plans, such as the performance of the car, road conditions and the weather. Sometimes a calm high-riding full moon would dominate the sky as they travelled, but other nights they could be battling through lashing rain or even snow storms. Always determined to get home, even if only for a few hours, the band members could be putting their keys in their door locks at all hours, in pitch dark or at dawn. At least they would be back in their own home fresh from new triumphs, or more likely exhausted from new conquests. For much of the time it was like playing a part in James Joyce's *Finnegan's Wake...* disturbing nocturnal visitations.

The wives became a mother and a father to any children as well as playing hostess to 'practising' sessions. Sutherland Street or the McKelvey house at Hepburn Street were the usual venues for these sessions, and it was at these times the band developed an eerie rapport which transferred to their performances. On the unusual occasion of Jimmy making a mistake the whole band made it with him.

Sandy Tulloch recalls taking a break from a medical tour to drop in and say hello to Jimmy and the band an hour before they were due to broadcast from Glasgow. When he asked George McKelvey what they would be playing, the answer was 'Don't know yet.' Sandy found this hard to believe. Surely they had rehearsed and rehearsed until they reached a satisfactory standard? It was certainly true that separate tunes were practised constantly, but programmes – no. Just before they were due to go on Jimmy casually said 'We'll start wi this, follow wi that – an then we'll see...' and it worked. Without any fuss, after the broadcast, they roped Owney's drums onto the roof of the car, packed themselves in and headed home.

After his demob. in 1946, Sandy Tulloch renewed his visits to Sutherland Street and found 'the same living room crowded with box players, fiddlers and would-be composers; the same welcome and generosity.' He recalls, 'The country dance world was really booming at that time, good new tunes were in great demand. Later on I thought that the quest for new or "rediscovered" dances got a little out of hand – it was hard work to commit hundreds of dances to memory. Most of the bands played from memory; seldom had anyone a sheet of music in front of them.'

Rushing here, playing their selection, rushing there, the band members barely had time to catch their breath. George McKelvey once said to his cousin David Phillips, 'It wasn't only Jimmy who had the reputation of never smiling in those days, but the whole band. Often we were playing like we were hypnotised, maybe having had only one night's sleep in three.'

It is probably just as well that the band's programmes were not made up solely of long sequences of dreamy waltzes, but were liberally sprinkled with rousing marches and reels. It could be said that the pattern of the way of life for the rest of the band's career was set in the first full-time year, but more was to come.

The band were contracted to make their first recordings in London, and George's sister provided their overnight accommodation. In 1946 recordings were made in soft wax and could not be played back immediately. The length had to be just right but with Jimmy and the band there was never any trouble over quality or timing. Neither did they tie up the recording studios or require extra time from the engineers for remakes. Such was their professional efficiency that they took less than a day to record their first batch of six records, which meant twelve sides. On the same day the engineer in an adjoining studio was applauding himself on having finally managed to produce just *one* record with another group.

It was not simply a case of Jimmy Shand and his band turning up and doing a job; they were the best in the business and this was particularly important when it came to live broadcasting. 'Who's Jimmy Shand?' was the reaction of Ronnie Calder, who was the Assistant Music Director at the BBC when he first heard them in 1946. Right from their very first broadcast with him, Jimmy and the band gained his considerable respect. He recalled, 'What a master of timing Jimmy was! Broadcasts were live then and it was always a great pleasure looking after one of his programmes for you knew he would get everything right and always finish tidily in musical fashion. And absolutely unflappable; a rock in an emergency.'

One Saturday afternoon, a Scots country dance band was involved in a crash on the way to Glasgow to do a Saturday night half hour. Ronnie phoned Jimmy and asked if he could help, he was desperate. Jimmy said he would do what he could although he knew that some of the lads might be at the football. One way and another he got everybody together and rushed to the studio with barely enough time for a sound balance. Bang on time the broadcast started and none of the listeners were aware that Jimmy and the band had stepped in at the last minute and substituted perfectly without any time for preparation. Ronnie Calder continued:

> Never any trouble due to temperament; nothing was too much to ask of them... When General Overseas wanted a programme to go out at 9.30 a.m., Jimmy and the band were there. They must have been up at the crack of dawn to make sure of arriving in time, for it was the depths of winter with black ice on the roads. Yet I have seldom been aware of such a feeling of immense vitality as I got from their playing that morning.
>
> Their dependability was a great comfort to production staff. Artistes in general are the most unpunctual of people. Not Jimmy; oh, maybe it often meant exceeding the speed limit to make it - but make it he would, you could depend on that.

By this time Erskine had gone back to his piano lessons and was doing quite well - but not so far as Jimmy was concerned. The evening before a pupil's exhibition illustrated a typical husband–son–wife situation: 'Na, na, lauddie, ye're no gettin the thing at a'; Ye havena been practisin. Anne, ye should have seen that he...' 'He has so been practisin! An he can play real guid...' 'Well, he's certainly no guid enough tae play at thae concert if that's the best he can dae!' 'It's wi you an the way ye stand ower him. He can so play guid - an he WILL play at the concert!' And he did, without letting teacher or parents down!

In 1947 Jimmy was finally persuaded to take a holiday and set off for Bridge of Allan with Anne and the boys. Jimmy never liked holidays other than at home, and unfortunately on this rare vacation he broke his ankle playing cricket with Erskine. This meant a lay-off of thirteen weeks and ensured he had even less time for going off on holiday after that.

He was able to keep an engagement for a Scottish dance music session with the BBC. When the band arrived at the BBC studios at Queen Margaret Drive in Glasgow, Jimmy asked George McKelvey to go ahead and find out which studio they were in. The astonished Ronnie Calder quickly told them they were supposed to be in the Edinburgh studios. Ronnie was nothing if not resourceful and removed a female artiste from a studio and installed Jimmy and the band. The young lady was heard wandering down the corridor bitterly muttering to herself that it must be great to be one of Ronnie's pals. A link-up was quickly set up with Edinburgh and to top it all the whole programme was recorded in London.

This was the year that Sandy Tulloch, having gone to work in Glasgow, was appointed visiting eye specialist to Argyll and the Inner Hebrides and 'met many enthusiasts and played a great deal, especially round about Oban, where we formed a quartet which came to be known as the Taynuilt Occasionals.' Whenever he could manage it he teamed up with other players in Glasgow and played for various Scottish Country Dance Society branches.

David and Erskine

After a broadcast in Glasgow one night, Jimmy popped down to Sandy's house in Scotstoun for a private word. 'Maybe it's just because Erskine was sae quick at pickin things up that maks it seem that David is, well a bit slow. I tell Anne that nae doot he'll catch up – a' bairns are no the same... Sandy, I want yer opinion straight...' Jimmy asked. Sandy replied, 'To be frank Jim, I've been wondering when you'd bring the subject round...' His explanation was sympathetic, but cautious, and 'best to see your own doctor. Now you'll do that, Jim?' he urged.

When both Erskine and David were born Dr Kirkland had been in attendance and he counselled Jimmy and Anne that the main thing was for parents to love their child and advised them there was a great deal of support available. There was no doubt that David was loved and wanted and a vital part of the family, and it was a considerable relief for Jimmy and Anne having faced up to the facts.

In 1947, Britain experienced such severe weather during the winter that it was referred to as 'The Great Blizzard'. Having fulfilled an engagement at Innerwick, Jimmy and the band packed the car expecting to head back to Dundee. The roads could not be used and they were marooned in the local hotel for four days and nights with only the clothes they were wearing. Six other hotel guests were also snowed up but their dismay and frustration was considerably eased by some unexpected impromptu entertainment.

By this time Johnny Knight, the pianist, was finding it difficult to play at all the band's engagements and keep his job in the printing trade. He recalled, 'Many's the time I've played from 7 p.m. to 4 a.m. then off to start a day's work at 7 a.m.' When he left, Harry Forbes played for a while before Norrie Whitelaw joined the band.

Norrie had never really wanted to 'go to the piano.' He felt it was one of life's great conspiracies against him that *his* mother had been offered a piano for £3 just when he was the right age for learning. To make matters worse Mrs Young, the pianoforte teacher, lived just around the top of the street and her fees were very reasonable. He was a boy who should have been involved in some boisterous chase or kickabout, or gaming for cigarette cards while drawing on an illicit Woodbine hiding in some seldom-frequented tenement passage. He felt a sissy sitting indoors doh–ray–me-ing.

Eventually, despite his resistance, an expertise developed which engaged his interest and he finally began to enjoy music.

He started work in a foundry as a hammer boy, but in the evenings he and a drummer friend of his would be the entire band hammering out waltzes and foxtrots at fourpenny or sixpenny dances in various small halls. By the time he became a blacksmith tradesman he had moved up the musical scale playing piano at the Forfar Palais with John Patterson's resident band. He was very happy when the chance to play with Jimmy arose.

The band was booked by the BBC to play in the New Year from Dundee's City Square with Ronnie Calder as the producer. After the broadcast was over, Ronnie went back to Sutherland Street to celebrate, 'and there would seem to be hundreds of folk in the little living room, yet always room for more... Mrs Shand seldom got a minute to herself for looking after the company – and always a seemingly inexhaustible reserve of boiled ham.'

Success after success meant Jimmy and the band played even more often and further away. Their venues included theatres, great public halls and ballrooms, castles and even palaces. They had opened the doors of the hall of fame, and the world danced in after them. One year seemed to flow into another without anybody noticing.

In 1949 Jimmy got in touch with Sandy Tulloch and said he was thinking about designing a new, special accordion. He asked if they could talk about it after one of the band's broadcasts in Glasgow. Sandy remembers the evening well. 'The new instrument was to be much larger than the original, with a wider range of treble keys, full bass side, with couplers on both treble and bass. The cost was to be astronomical for the time – almost £200 – but I decided I would get one if it could be arranged.' The specifications were duly sent off to Hohner in Germany to see what they could produce.

The band's records were now almost permanent fixtures in the Top Ten with sales of 50,000 and more. Jimmy had certainly come a long way from the wee laddie haen a choon doon at the dykes at East Wemyss on his dad's box, but perhaps in the most important way he had not *really* changed at all!

Male nurse Andy Sutherland, a neighbour in Sutherland Street, recalls:

On a fine night he'd come out and sit on the garden dyke, and he'd play. Often he'd persuade big John Tosh, the police sergeant from number 25, to bring his accordion out for a duet. Before you knew it all the neighbours were out and there was an eightsome reel in full swing. The music and the word would got around, attracting more and more people, until some nights the street would be completely blocked and traffic further up brought to a standstill. There was a permanent understanding that any time the wife and I had a few friends in we'd only to knock on Jimmy's door and he'd be over right away to entertain them. The Shands were the best of neighbours in every way. Like Jim, my missus had trouble with her stomach and they used to swap tablets and powders. Jim loved pottering about in his garage, working on a car or a motorbike, or making toys for the laddies.

We had a son then ages with his David, and the two of them were great pals, as at home in each other's home as in their own. Many a time David would be in playing with my

Sutherland Street, Dundee

Andrew when we'd hear his mother calling for him and
he'd plead 'Dinna tell her I'm here!' he'd be that absorbed in
their little ploys. I helped Jim with little jobs on his vehicles
when I could; went with him on a few trips and did a bit of
relief driving. I think it helped Anne and him a bit to see
how my wee boy unreservedly accepted theirs as a
completely normal playmate, and I was glad to be able to
use my own specialised experience to remind him that
David was a high grade handicapped child. Often Jimmy
would step across from his garage to show me some toy he
was making; or perhaps he would be preoccupied in the
making of something else. 'What dae ye think o this Andra?'
he would ask. 'Dy-dy-dydill-aye-di-dy-dy-dy...' I was
privileged to be first to hear many of his compositions.

John Tosh, the police sergeant, who would have easily seen
through insincere social behaviour or false modesty, once said
to Alan Dunsmore, a journalist friend of Jimmy's, 'Y'know, we
havna got the right focus on Jimmy Shand. He's no jist a braw
box player – an yon music has *body* in it, it's better than a diet o
meat. When he plays *Rowan Tree* ye can see it growin. Even
when my Doog was a bairn on my knee, he'd sit quiet when
any other band was on the wireless – but wi Jimmy's he'd jump
up and doon like a mad ane an near fa aff! But it's no just that
Jimmy's a braw box player – here for a whilie an then awa –
Shand's pert o Scottish history. He'll live lang after he's deid.'

On a rare free day Jimmy and big John went to visit some
mutual friends in the village of Errol. It was inevitable that
Jimmy would play a tune or two. On hearing the music a
woman from across the way called in wondering if Mr Shand
could possibly spare a minute to say hello to her daughter
Margaret. It seems that Margaret, bedridden for more than a
year, had been a Jimmy Shand fan for a long while. The
'minute' turned into a three-hour concert which attracted the
local bobby from his beat, a cattleman from his byre, the
blacksmith from his anvil as well as other friends and
neighbours. They all crowded upstairs in the sick girl's room
and were there when the doctor called. He stayed to hear a few
tunes before he had to leave. As he was going out the door,

Margaret's mother asked why he had not left any medicine. 'He could see the lassie's no needin any the day. An her singin...,' John said at the time. 'A drop of Shand's better than a' yer tablets!' he added, seriously.

On the way home Jimmy said to John, 'That's the kind o thing that maks my job seem real worthwhile. Ye ken, I'd rather hae been in there than in the Albert Hall.' There wasn't the slightest doubt that he meant it.

In 1950 he appeared as a guest soloist at the All Britain Accordion Championships Grand Evening concert in the Central Hall, Westminster. The Championships had been revived the previous year and sponsored by the National Accordion Organisation of Great Britain. It was a big event as there were classes for solo, duet, trio/quartet, bands from junior and elementary to advanced, and amateur to open. Area winners went to London to compete in the finals, and the Grand Evening Concert displayed not only the talents of the newly elected Champions, but also invited celebrities from Britain and the continent (of Europe).

On this famous London stage Jimmy, the only busker among the elite of British and Continental Champions, his head turned away much of the time as if in distaste at his playing, stopped the show. His selection was: *Inverness Gathering, Braes o Tulliment, John Cheap the Chapman.* Not surprisingly, he was invited back for the following year!

In 1951, several packages arrived from the Hohner factory in Germany. Sandy Tulloch explains:

> The new instruments arrived, the first models of the Shand Morino. Everything was up to expectations except the 'answering' of the bass. The tone was magnificent but we both sensed a slight lag in response to the bellows action. I think it was perhaps that the original Shand Special had been such a remarkable instrument. We must have got used to it, however, as we have played this model ever since, and many more have been made and supplied for button key enthusiasts since these first two models were delivered. My faithful old Scandalli found a home with the Hawthorn Accordion Band, and, I hope, gave good service.

It was about this time that Jimmy, Ian Powrie and Jim
Cameron came out to Scotstoun to supper after one of the
broadcasts. Ian always remembers that night because of the
number of salmon sandwiches he managed to put away.
Jimmy was off duty and feeling relaxed, and off we went
into a 'continental' session; it was great fun, and we played
on for quite a time. However, Jim Cameron was sitting
quietly with his fiddle on his knee and eventually said 'Fit
aboot playin something we can a' play?' and away we went
into some of the strathspeys that made *him* such a distinctive
player.

Jimmy went down to London again for the All Britain
Accordion Championships, this time playing for a team of
dancers. The Souvenir Programme, which presumably based its
comments on impressions gained in 1950, said:

> ...Bringing a further individual touch to the programme and
> representing as he does a mighty accordion stronghold

Jimmy and the band with dancers at the
All Britain Accordion Championships, 1951
(*Dancers l-r: George Garland, Ellen Spence, Margaret Pert, Mrs Stewart, Nan Hill*)

north of the Border, is Scots accordionist Jimmy Shand,
whose own genial personality on stage reflects the sturdy joviality
of the Scots songs and dances in whose interpretation he is
the unchallenged master.

You will notice the words in italics. In the years to come, the
Championships featured Jimmy Shand and his Band and
Highland Country Dancers, and typical of the programme
notes were, '...Accordion Day would hardly be complete
without a contribution from Jimmy Shand.'

His music was now setting feet tapping all over Britain as well
as further afield; the Shand name and sound was heard widely
overseas by the early 50s. Records were selling well, not only in
Canada, Australia and New Zealand, but also in Paris and
Singapore. For example, a radio station in Moosejaw,
Saskatchewan, Canada, had a weekly half hour of Shand
recordings. Records were being bought by Scots exiles all over
the world and pounced upon by anyone on a trip home. They
were despatched by friends and relations in answer to urgent
pleas from clubs, societies, yachts, naval bases, barracks,
aerodromes, mansions, penthouses, hunting lodges, adobes
and a wide variety of outposts. The very precise rhythms of the
reel, the strathspey, the schottische and the polka drifted out
from grass shacks, igloos and through the bead curtains of
oriental music shops.

Igloos? There were probably not many Scots exiles living in
igloos, but it is a known fact that many Eskimos loved and
bought Jimmy's music and records. A hundred years earlier,
whaling crews from Dundee had taught them the dances and
how to manipulate the squeeze box. To this day many Eskimo
women still play the accordion. Sometimes exiles reacted in
dramatic ways to Jimmy's music. A young emigrant in Canada,
who had never known the meaning of home-sickness, heard a
record of Jimmy playing reels: half way through it she was
crying, and after it had finished she promptly went out and
booked a passage on the next ship home!

The listening and buying public were now attuned to

'Jimmy Shand and his Band', and the big successes were attributed to the group. This was a pity in some ways as, although a wonderful rapport existed within the group, Jimmy was now only heard as one of the boys. This blending-in suited an undemonstrative person such as Jimmy, but it has to be regretted as a loss to the public of one of the greatest individualistic instrumental soloists of his generation. Most band leaders regularly took centre stage in front of their groups and demonstrated their virtuosity. Perhaps Jimmy should have done this, but being Jimmy he didn't. He was quite unique as a soloist but also the most reserved. No other accordion player ever got so much from the instrument with such a minimum movement of the bellows; there was nothing flashy or flourishing about his style. Most of his solo playing was now restricted to performing for charitable causes or visiting old folks' clubs or hospitals.

One of his rare public appearances as a soloist, combined with his less than flamboyant style, led to an interesting encounter with one of his audience. He was appearing at the Newcastle Empire and a churlish young man, who had obviously had a drink or two, demanded to see him backstage. Jimmy allowed him to be let into his dressing room and asked him what he wanted. Jimmy recalls the conversation:

'Just want to complain, you're taking in the public. We paid to hear you *play* you know!' the man blustered.
    'Well?' asked Jimmy.
    'Only you're *not* playing. You don't take me in! And you haven't even got the sense to make it look more realistic! Anybody could tell you're *miming*,' the man continued.
    'Think so?' Jimmy enquired.
    The man shouted, 'I know so! Must think the public's stupid – why man you've hardly been opening the bellows!'
    'A' richt laddie,' Jimmy said as he strapped on the box. 'Watch closely now, mind.' With one hand he held closed all but one of the accordion pleats, with the other he launched into the tumultuous arpeggios of the melodeonist's showpiece the *High Level Hornpipe* at speed.

The young man was stunned and his mouth opened wider than the bellows. With profuse apologies he backed out of the dressing room quite in awe with what he had witnessed.

Later he sent Jimmy a letter apologising for his behaviour and expressing his admiration and enthusiasm.

One of the titles affectionately applied to Jimmy and the band, because of their record sales and their many broadcasts, was Top Teuchter Ensemble. While Jimmy's economical playing style dumbfounded an audience, a personal appearance of the band sometimes caused surprise. The five of them would arrive for a dance or concert and find up to twelve places laid for them in the ante-room. On one occasion in a remote village hall they overheard one committee member indignantly whisper to another, 'By goad he's only brought half the band!' The enthusiastic turning up of the volume on the wireless possibly gave the impression that the band was much bigger.

In 1952, however, the numbers in the band nearly did not matter, as they all came within a grace note of switching to harps.

Seven

The big black Packard saloon car, with Jimmy at the wheel, was running smoothly on the road from London to Elsdon, in Northumberland, where the band were booked to play at a function. The car was purring sweetly as it should: £300 had recently been spent on a new engine, gearbox, tyres and lamps. The sixteen gallon tank had been filled at Doncaster, a mile back down the road, and everything should have been fine on the early November evening... but it wasn't!

Thinking there was condensation on the glass Jimmy rubbed the inside of the windscreen. As things were not clearing Jimmy said to the boys in the band, 'Gettin a bit foggy, lads.' 'Seems pretty clear fae here, Jim,' said Owney McCabe, looking out of the rear window. Puzzled by this Jimmy said, 'Well it's definitely... wait a minute, it seems tae be *inside*...!' Quickly slamming the brakes on he shouted, 'Oot, quick as ye can!'

Once everybody was out, Jimmy lifted the bonnet of the car and jumped back as a tongue of flame threatened to engulf his wrist. A major 'save-the-instruments' plan was put into operation. A knife was produced to slash the ropes holding Owney's drum kit and John White's double bass on the roof rack. All the instruments were taken away from the road and laid in a field as black, pungent smoke billowed from the car.

Norrie Whitelaw set off up the road to warn traffic of the situation. Someone put in an emergency telephone call to the Fire Brigade, but as the band watched from a distance the smoke got thicker and spread higher and wider. On the road a short distance away, the driver of a little car saw Norrie too late, and swerved, grazing him and knocking him into the ditch. The car carried on up a bank and stopped inches from a tree – the young couple inside could not get out as the doors had jammed. Jimmy and the rest of the band rushed to the scene, released the shaken young people and ascertained that, fortunately, Norrie had only bruised a hip.

By this time a fire engine had arrived, but almost immediately another one appeared from a different direction. The smoking car had stopped on the boundary between two areas. While the fire crews discussed the seemingly impossible situation, the smoke continued to darken the sky. WHOOSH! Flames forty feet high suddenly shot into the air and enveloped the large car. All Jimmy and the band could do was sadly watch as the windows cracked and melted, the brand new tyres swelled hideously, and the metal twisted bizarrely. 'Pity aboot the bairns' toys, Owney,' Jimmy commented quietly, thinking about the glove puppets they had bought in London and left in the car. While the fire brigade doused the car, Jimmy fondly remembered how he had always considered it was the best vehicle he had ever possessed for transporting the band and instruments around the country.

The band's transportation problems were solved by the purchase of a little brown bus they named 'Bonnie Dundee',

The band with the burnt out Packard car

decorated with the opening bars of the tune painted on the side. Although Jimmy was fond of driving, he took on ex-taxi driver Andy Gow as regular driver. This meant the whole band could at least get a little sleep on long journeys, although if Andy was in a hurry the naps could be, and were, fitful.

Although Jimmy was having wonderful success, he continually worried about the length of time he spent away from home. Despite the fact he would always get back to Dundee as quickly as possible after an engagement was over, he was very conscious of the great demands made upon Anne bringing up the boys. If it hadn't been for her wonderful capability and enthusiasm, Jimmy would not have had the confidence to carry on. Erskine was progressing very well on the continental button accordion under the tutorship of Billy Grogan – and David, like all growing boys, was into everything.

David Phillips remembered one occasion in the Shand's house in Sutherland Street when he was painting the kitchenette. Before leaving for an engagement in England Jimmy turned and said, 'Mind the lauddie now, Anne.'

'Of coorse, of coorse, I'll pay attention, awa ye go now, the baund'll be waiting for ye. David'll be a' richt – I'll mind yer lauddie,' Anne said, accompanying Jimmy to the door. As she cleared up the breakfast dishes after Jimmy had gone she said, 'Aye – him an his lauddie!'

After lunch the phone rang. 'There he is,' she said to David and answered, 'Aye, aye Jimmy, he's a' richt.' As she put the phone down she said, 'What did I tell ye? "Is the lauddie a' richt?" Always his first words nae matter whaur he phones fae.'

When Jimmy was looking for a replacement fiddler in 1952 he discovered, from the dozens of applications, just how many people wanted to play in a Shand band. Jimmy asked his old friend Jim Barrie if he would help go through them.

Jimmy remembers Jim saying, 'Ye want me tae help get ye a fiddler?'

'That's what these letters are a' aboot. Would ye hae a look through them when ye have time?' Jimmy asked.

Jim Barrie pushed the letters to one side. 'I'll tell you about a fiddler,' he said. Nae need tae gae through this lot.'

And that's the way Syd Chalmers became the Shand band's new fiddler – and its youngest member at 32 – before Jimmy had even heard him play.

Bonnie Dundee

Jim Barrie, an expert fiddler in his own right, was certainly not selling Jimmy a pig-in-a-poke, having known Syd since 1933. The son of Forfar Pipe Band's Pipe Major, the young Syd had entered the Alyth Festival and was waiting to compete when Jim spoke to him and gave him some words of encouragement. When he discovered the laddie in short breeks was only fifteen and had entered the open class he expressed his surprise and asked to hear him play. After hearing Syd play the haunting slow march *Dark Lochnagar*, Jim put his hand on the laddie's shoulder and sighed, 'Aye!' Syd won the competition and two years later was Scottish Fiddle Champion. For the next sixteen years Syd travelled round about earning his living through music, even learning to play the clarinet and saxophone to increase his chances of getting engagements. He was back home when he heard of Jim Barrie's recommendation and very happily joined the Shand band.

Jim Barrie did more than provide Jimmy with a fiddler; he also frequently recommended tunes. On one unbelievably lucky day he was in the right place at the right time to dramatically increase his stock of music. He worked with Dundee Cleansing Department and was observing a load of rubbish being tipped for destruction, when instinctively he shouted STOP! What he had seen was an obviously old book, but it is likely that only a fiddler's eye would have noticed the faded name on the cover – Gow... The book was retrieved and handled with care. What Jim Barrie had in his hands was a volume of *Niel Gow's Repository of 1804*, the legendary fiddler's collection of 300 tunes!

On Jimmy's behalf Jim Barrie was soon dipping into the rare publication. On one occasion there was a request for no less than 'ten new marches.' Jimmy didn't read music but after Jim Barrie had whistled each of the selected marches three times, they were permanently embedded in the famous Shand memory. They were not only remembered, but they underwent the unexplainable transmutation which put the Jimmy Shand stamp on them from the first playing. Dr Herbert Wiseman, Scottish music chief of the BBC, recognised this 'uniqueness' and commented on it in a Clydebank lecture in 1953. He said, 'In the matter of Scottish dance music, Jimmy Shand has a lilt in his playing that none of the others ever had.'

In 1953, when he was eight years old, David Shand developed a severe attack of pneumonia and was rushed to King's Cross Hospital. Dr Jameson reported at the time on David's condition.

> Thanks to the availability of antibiotic remedies he made an excellent recovery, and after about a fortnight he was able to return home. In the same year, however, he fell ill again with a respiratory infection... This happened just a few days before Christmas... Jimmy brought a tape of himself and his band so that we could have music in the ward on Christmas Day...
> 'Just watch David's face when he hears it,' and it was a

great joy to see the laddie's face light up as he listened with rapt attention. Jimmy and Anne had showered quite expensive toys on David, and when the time came for him to go home Jimmy insisted that all the toys should remain in the ward for the other kids.

'You see, Bill, we bought twa o everything – the same things are waitin for him at hame.'

This was a very typical gesture…

In 1953 Alan Dunsmore, a journalist with D.C. Thomson & Co. Ltd in Dundee wrote a series of articles which were published in the *People's Journal*. The series was well received and inspired readers to write to the newspaper. They included the following:

> I must congratulate you on the wonderful idea of publishing the life story of Jimmy Shand. I have known and admired him from the first day he set foot in Forbes' music shop in King's Road Dundee. Such was the charm of his playing that the office staff (of which I was the head), crept to the top of the stair to listen, entranced. As a rule we tried hard to shut out the weird and awful sounds which some prospective clients made when trying out a box, but not this time. We just couldn't get enough. After that we were his most ardent fans and when he joined the staff we followed him all over the district in bus loads to encourage him. Our one concern then was to make him smile – he was too shy to do even that on a platform. He still is the shyest of men among strangers and hates all fuss and palaver, but he has a heart of gold and an integrity of spirit not often met these days. He has never forgotten his friends of the old days, and gives up many hours to their pleasure of listening to his inimitable, lilting music. He has many a time played to my own mother at her express wish when she was able to enjoy an evening's entertainment and, at 92 she still remembers those days.
>
> *His playing was so infectious that it made even my parrot dance and 'hooch' like a real Scot!* That used to make our solemn Jimmy Shand laugh all right. Great prowess to his fingers, and may he long give pleasure to fellow Scots the world over.
>
> Isobel M. Reid, Dundee

> I find your articles about Jimmy Shand so interesting that I send them each week to SHAPE Headquarters near Paris, where

Jimmy has become almost a legend. Why? Because for years a large gathering of people of six nationalities – Frenchmen, Belgians, Dutchmen, Luxembourgers, Americans and of course Englishmen and Scots – have regular weekly Scottish Country Dancing evenings… all to the music of Jimmy Shand's records. Whenever any of his records are required they are flown over by an RAF plane from the UK, and so popular has Jimmy become that when any of the officers or men are posted back to their respective countries they often take a parcel of his records back with them.

The foreigners have great difficulty in pronouncing the names of the Scottish dances – *Strip the Willow* is 'la Streep', *Dashing White Sergeant* is 'Le Dasheeng', and the *Eightsome Reel* the 'Weetsome'. But as soon as you put on a Jimmy Shand record they know right away which dance it is. If Jimmy ever goes to Paris he will get a great reception.

Ben G. Forbes, Dundee

It is with great pleasure that I take this opportunity of expressing what Jimmy Shand means to me and many others here in hospital. When we hear his music we forget our troubles and it seems to give us fresh courage… thanks for publishing 'The Jimmy Shand Story'. I am proud to be the bearer of the same name.

James Shand, Stokemandeville Hospital, Aylesbury

What the many thousands of fans who had seen him, or the millions who had heard him play, did not realise was that, for quite a while, Jimmy had been coping with disturbing indications of wear and tear. His digestive system, which had been delicate since his early days as a miner, had certainly not been helped by the rushing all over Britain in all weathers, sometimes playing half the night and travelling the rest, snatching food if and when he could.

It had been suggested by his doctor, quite strongly, that he should make a personal appearance at another type of 'theatre' and Jimmy agreed to do this, but did not make a definite booking. One day in 1953, when he was sitting at home talking to Alan Dunsmore about the newspaper articles, he suddenly felt the time had come for him to keep the appointment!

As Alan drove Jimmy to Dundee Royal Infirmary it seemed

at last that the unruly stomach would be dealt with. Certainly Jimmy was operated on in the hospital – to take out his appendix. His stomach problem would have to wait for another day!

Jimmy and the band had travelled the length and breadth of mainland Britain before deciding, in 1954, to accept some of the many invitations to go to Ireland. What may have seemed strange – that a Scottish country dance band should be popular in Ireland – proved to be an outstanding success, and a severe test of Andy Gow's driving ability. They arrived in Belfast on Saturday 11 September and once the 'Bonnie Dundee' had disembarked, they sped along the road to Dublin to take part in a couple of broadcasts.

The tour had started in a hectic way and was to become even more so. Twenty-two 'one night stands' involved travelling 3,000 miles up and down and back and forth in less than a logical sequence around Ireland – what the song calls 'A little bit of heaven that once fell from out the sky'. Jimmy modestly thought that the bus passing and re-passing through various districts kept the band's name before the public, and it may have had a little to do with the near-riotous enthusiasm with which they were greeted everywhere. However, the main reason for the wonderful reception was Jimmy, the band, and their music.

A pipe band playing *Scotland the Brave* welcomed the bus when it arrived at Cappagh White, near Tipperaray. There was such a crowd round the 'Bonnie Dundee' that Jimmy and the band had the greatest difficulty getting the door open. The organisers of the evening's dance had dispensed with a hall and erected a giant marquee, to hold 2,000 people. More than 10,000 would-be dancers turned up, many having travelled up to 50 miles to get there. For a while the dance committee tried to dissuade possible gatecrashers by patrolling outside the bulging walls armed with shillelaghs, but eventually they realised their attempts were futile and the canvas walls were rolled up out of the way, the marquee roof flapping in the wind marking the ridiculous attempt to confine the performance of

Jimmy and the band to a select 2,000.

The dance finished at 3 a.m., and Norrie Whitelaw, who had battled hard all evening to hold the piano steady with one hand against the crush of bodies while playing with the other, breathed a huge sigh of relief. The great swell of autograph hunters kept Jimmy busy until well after 6 o'clock. As far as his fans were concerned, Jimmy could have signed himself 'Mr Scotland' and they would not have complained.

The hundreds, the thousands, were all individuals to Jimmy who was still in awe that people gave their time and money to come and see him.

In a little place called Glenfarne, the early comers to the dance were passing the time practising their footwork to gramophone records. Sitting at the side, a teenage girl wearing a calliper sat by herself watching the activities, hoping she could cope with the crush at the end of the evening to get Jimmy's autograph. She had settled in her own mind that girls with her disability never get asked to dance. Suddenly, incredibly, standing in front of her was Jimmy himself, who with humble courtesy bent forward and asked her, 'Will ye hae this ane wi me?' The rest of the evening was a blur as she was borne away in an old fashioned waltz by the maestro himself.

In Cork, where the band was booked to appear in the celebrated Arcadia Ballroom, Jimmy got a visit from the police. The crowds in the street were causing such an obstruction that the local constabulary approached Jimmy in his hotel room hours before the dance was due to begin, asking if he would agree to the ballroom doors opening early to clear the congestion. The hall held 1,400 people comfortably, but some enterprising Irishman had sold 3,000 tickets!

A policeman took Andy Gow aside and explained their plan of action. 'We'll let them in at the front and when it starts to get a bit too crowded we'll start lettin them out the back!'

During the same evening Andy remembers struggling through to the buffet to get a cup of tea and being faced by the sweating harassed waitress who snapped at him menacingly.

'An it'll be one of THEM now, ye are, is it? Well I hope Jimmy Shand stays in Scotland for evermore!'

The last engagement in Ireland, in Tralee, was another episode which imprinted itself in Andy's memory. The bus had over 300 miles to cover to meet the boat in Belfast, and the dance did not finish until after 3 a.m. After the packing up and the autographs, Andy knew he would have to get a move on. The bus was racing through the Irish countryside, when suddenly near Ninagh, it was brought to a halt. Meandering along the road was a herd of cattle, not just any herd, but one large enough to do justice to a lavish western epic in the cinema. The cattle dominated the road for the next twenty miles, forcing 'Bonnie Dundee' to travel at 5 mph. The little brown bus reached the boat with three minutes to spare.

After the Irish tour the heavy schedule of engagements continued from the Shetland Isles to the Channel Isles. By 1955, 'Bonnie Dundee' was covering over 30,000 miles each year. Everyone in showbusiness agrees that one night stands are the most exhausting way to perform, and many of Jimmy's friends were concerned at his work rate. Archie McCulloch, the journalist and broadcaster who often compered Scottish shows, wondered at the time, 'if he takes too much out of himself chasing up and down the country? His boys may be in Inverness one night and Carlisle the next, and so on. Practically every week they make at least one trip to England. Take it from me, there's no bigger box office attraction in Scotland. Whether he is scheduled to appear at a small hall in the Highlands or the Usher Hall in Edinburgh, the hall is booked out hours after the first announcement.'

Archie went on to point out that it did not make any sense from the purely commercial point of view to bother with the smaller engagements in the out-of-the-way places, when he could guarantee to pack the biggest halls in the land. He would make more money and have an easier time if he confined his work to playing for a week at a time in the big theatres.

Jimmy, although seeing the point, did not subscribe to what

was being suggested. So far as he was concerned it was the organisers and committees of the small dances who had made his band popular and he certainly was not going to go high-hat and let them down now. When he knew a small organisation could not afford to pay him a big fee, he charged according to their limit.

Archie McCulloch again commented, 'Whatever way we look at it we must salute a man who sacrifices a lot of money – and energy – in order to give a helping hand to the small promoter who was good to him in the days gone by. We could do with many more Jimmy Shands...'

In the spring of 1955 Jimmy and the band did take a week's engagement at the Palace Theatre in Dundee. More than 17,000 people attended, which was more than any other show had drawn in the same number of performances in the 80 years of the theatre's history. Eric Page, the theatre manager said afterwards, 'It was the biggest sell-out we ever had. All week we were trying to persuade him to play solo, we never managed it. Jimmy never wants any personal credit.'

In June of the same year he kept his date with the operating theatre when he was rushed to hospital with a perforated ulcer. He went to Fernbrae, a private nursing home, and it embarrassed him as to what people might think. He explained to his friends, 'Dinna get the idea that I think I'm better than other folk, the ordinary hospital would've done me, same as anybody else, but there's the band tae consider. It's quicker this way, an we can get this thing ower an done wi afore oor busy season starts.'

He was showered with get well cards from all over but for one critical week he needed all the well-wishing he could get. His chances were estimated at no more than fifty-fifty and only his wife Anne was allowed in to see him.

As soon as he was well enough, the visitors began to arrive in droves. A long distance lorry driver on his way north from work in Northumberland, parked his great ten-wheeled vehicle outside the nursing home. He had heard about Jimmy's illness and decided to break his journey to say hello to the man who'd played at the best hop his village had ever had. Jimmy's bedroom became almost like a royal audience chamber, as among his first visitors were the leaders of countless other Scottish music groups coming like courtiers paying homage to the king.

When Jimmy had been rushed into Fernbrae his weight had been 13 stone 10 pounds, but he was down to ten stone two weeks after the operation. 'I must have had a bloomin heavy belly,' he recalled, indicating that under the sombre façade there was a sense of humour.

By the end of July Jimmy was back on the bus again; after all he had ten radio programmes to record in London! By September he was off on his first tour across the Atlantic. Neil Kirk, the Dundee-born New York impresario, took a long while to arrange the tour as he knew that the money on offer to Jimmy, no matter how much it was, would not be enough to convince him to go. It was when Neil mentioned the tens of thousands of exiles who would love to hear and see Jimmy in the flesh that the deal was done. Jimmy remembered so many friends and neighbours from his younger days who had left their homes to go abroad. There were the proud men, not having Jimmy's gift, who stubbornly insisted on the right to earn a decent living and give their families a reasonable chance in life. They and their stout-hearted womenfolk were prepared to travel thousands of miles for even the likelihood of an opportunity. When he thought of the Gordons, the Sutherlands and the Hannahs from Buckhaven and East Wemyss who had gone to Canada, Jimmy felt sure he would feel at home.

Union restrictions prevented the rest of the band going on tour, so Jimmy would have to perform solo as part of a Scottish Variety Show. The others in the party were the celebrated tenor Robert Wilson, with his accompanist Tammas Fisher, Jack Anthony, Bertha Ricardo, Jimmy Neil and Margaret Mitchell.

There was one condition about the tour which made Jimmy pause for a moment, and that was the requirement to wear a kilt. It wasn't that he was worried about his legs – all those years of pushing and climbing down the pit or working as a navvy had developed strong muscles which could carry a kilt with a swagger – it was just that he had never considered it before. After agreeing to wear one he wondered which tartan he should have, as there was not a Shand weave. He chose the Anderson tartan, after Anne's maiden name, and had a length of it and some velvet material made up as his 'gauin abroad' outfit.

At Prestwick Airport it did not seem as if anybody was going anywhere. Bad weather delayed the tour party's flight from Saturday to Sunday. Eventually, as they were due to take off, an embarrassed official informed them there had been a mix-up with the reservations and all the seats were taken. If they agreed, they could travel in the comfortable and well stocked cocktail bar and all their refreshments would be free. One person who was delighted with the arrangement was Jack Anthony, as he was celebrating his birthday. The aircraft company did not lose much on Jimmy as his tipple was an orange juice, and besides, he slept through most of the journey. 'Not THE Jimmy Shand?' the excited customs officer at Montreal Airport exclaimed, when he saw the name on the accordion box. Thereafter, Jimmy had no problem going through the gate.

Despite the good omen, Jimmy wondered whether he had been wise to venture so far from home. Soon he had a very definite answer. The Massey Hall in Toronto was crammed with 4,000 people when he walked diffidently on to the stage, feeling a little lonely far fae hame and not sure if he was comfortable in a kilt. He needn't have worried, as Robert Wilson reported at the time. 'It was like a madhouse, in all my experience I never saw an artiste receive such a riotous reception.'

'Scottish Variety Show Rocks Hall at Opening' was the headline of a review in the following morning's paper. 'Top billing goes this time to accordionist Jimmy Shand, a tall, bald and dour Scotsman who, all evening long, scarcely cracked a smile, but his crisp, toe-tapping tunes exuded personality at every squeeze of the bellows ... he stole the show last night.' Later in the review there was a description of a Jack Anthony–

Bertha Ricardo sketch (dressed as a Spanish senorita, Bertha spoke in broken English): 'Don't you know the Queen's English?' asks Jack. 'No, senor.' 'Well she is...' This brought deafening applause, followed by, 'And her mither is Scottish!' which brought the house down. *You can't beat the old jokes!*

The one thing the tour wasn't was a series of one night stands. They played at the Massey Hall for three nights and in other places at least three and sometimes four nights.

A Vancouver newspaper carried the following advertisement promoting the show:

CALLING ALL SCOTS!
Dinna Miss the Grrrand
Opening Nicht of The Famous
White Heather Variety Concert

The same newspaper headlined its review the following day, 'Scots troupe wildly applauded for flow of sporrantaneous wit.'

Jimmy did not socialise very much with the rest of the troupe. It wasn't that he didn't like them or that he hid himself away; the truth is that he was always out and about whenever they stopped for a few days.

'Where are you away to now?' Jack Anthony would ask as Jimmy walked towards the door.

'Just awa tae see an auld schule pal I promised tae look up,' Jimmy replied.

Eventually when Jimmy came back to the hotel Jack would ask, 'And where have you been, Shand?'

'An auld freend! Just had tae visit, we were lauddies.'

'Jimmy, tell me something, is East Wemyss a very big place?'

'Na – Anything but, Jack, a wee bit place.'

'Well, it must have had a helluva big school wi a' the mates you've been gettin around!'

Jimmy remembers it was Neil Kirk who first made the comment but acknowledges that Jack Anthony kept the joke going.

At every theatre and hall they played, fans queued outside Jimmy's dressing room door after each performance to get his autograph and shake his hand. More often than not phrases like, 'An hoo's things in Buckhaven nooadays?' or 'Mind an tell them next time ye're back in Wemyss,' were exchanged. While he was discharging the messages from back home with which he was entrusted, Jimmy was being loaded with even more to take back.

Jimmy remembers a young man who introduced himself in Edmonton. He said his name was John Davidson and his father had been a Lochee scaffie (street sweeper) who used to do Jimmy's street.

'Oh aye, I mind o him noo. Wait noo – didn't his lauddie deliver oor milk?' Jimmy asked.

The man agreed and said *he* was the lauddie and he was now preparing to sit his final exams to become a minister.

Jimmy was visited at the Laurentian Hotel in Montreal by Alf Lawson, a miner friend from Denbeath. They had continued their friendship when Alf moved to Hepburn Street in Dundee. They talked about the time Jimmy had played at Alf's daughter's birthday party in North Street Hall and then Alf asked if Jimmy had time to go and see Mrs Lawson, as she wasn't well enough to come out. Although his schedule was tight Jimmy said, 'I'll be oot the morn, tell her.' Jimmy did go to see her, and after a private recital, promised her, 'An I'll look in an see ye again on oor way back.'

When the troupe returned to Montreal a few months later, Alf came to see him and Jimmy enquired about Mrs Lawson. Jimmy was saddened to hear that she had died, but was touched when Alf said she had made him promise to thank Jimmy again for cheering her up that day.

Jack Anthony told the story of how a Scots chambermaid at one hotel asked him one night if Jimmy would play a tune for her and some of the staff in one of the corridors. She said she had a lot of Shand records which her husband had collected before he died in the war. It was late, but when Jack asked Jimmy, he not only played he composed as well. Jack had written a lyric, the last line of which was *It's grand amang yer ain folk far, far from hame* which Jimmy set to music within five minutes. Margaret Mitchell sang it to Robert Wilson using the hotel's in-house telephone to his bedroom. The tenor expressed his delight at the new composition. As for the chambermaid, she was crying and smiling at the same time.

The tour continued: Ottawa, Port Arthur, Winnipeg, Saskatoon, Edmonton, Calgary and smaller places in between to Vancouver, then inland to Chulliwack and Kamloops 300 miles up the Fraser River. Over to Vancouver Island to play the main towns before coming back to the mainland and an 11-hour flight to Toronto. 'Like crossing the Atlantic again,' as Jimmy put it. Four shows in Toronto and on to London, Ontario and Windsor; then over the border to Philadelphia, New York and New Jersey. Jimmy had to leave the company and fly home after that in order to honour commitments and Anne, Erskine and David were at Prestwick to meet him.

When asked what he thought of it all, Jimmy replied, 'It was almost as if we'd never left Scotland. Everywhere ye heard the tongues o Fife, Aberdeen, Glesgie, Dundee an the Borders. We got a terrific reception wherever we went, an the hospitality was wonderful. Scots, Canadians and Americans alike gave us a great time. An there were folk that had gaun oot oer forty years ago still had their accents as if they'd just left Scotland.'

The crowds in Ireland request Jimmy's autograph

Eight

It was good to be home – but just for one day! Jimmy and the band set off on a series of one-night stands, taking in London, Eastbourne, London again, Market Harborough, Manchester and Ayr. On the day they got back from that short tour, they left for Whitley Bay, where Jimmy was presented with a portrait which had been painted by Wallace Lee, the secretary and treasurer of the Whitley Bay Scottish Country Dance Club. After the presentation the band moved on to Kirkintilloch and so it went on and on and on...

After the splendid hospitality and glamour of the North American tour it was, as far as Jimmy was concerned, a change to be 'back tae auld claes an paritch.' Moth balls were purchased to protect the kilt for another day and a decision was made to paint out the name on the wee broon band bus. 'Ach, it was just provin a nuisance,' Jimmy said.

While Jimmy was touring in the US and Canada, the Shand band fulfilled engagements in Britain as arranged. Talks were underway dealing with the possibility of television performances if and when they could be fitted in, as Jimmy and the band were heavily booked for 1956. Jimmy's stomach, or what was left of it, was fine and prospects looked rosy when suddenly, just before the band and himself were due to play at a dance which was to be broadcast from Perth City Hall, Jimmy collapsed. The nature of this sudden ailment was not as many people supposed, his stomach again, but more likely to have been profound fatigue or nervous exhaustion. In the best show business tradition the band played on without him that evening and for a few weeks until he felt fit enough to undertake some broadcasting work.

Despite his health scares and the constant '*take it a bit easier*' medical advice, Jimmy continued to respond to the never-ending call from his vast public to perform. The band and himself did a series of broadcasts called 'Personal Appearance', which involved travelling all over the country with Robert Wilson, Kathie Kay and Jimmy Neil. His records, which were often recorded and produced very quickly, were selling in vast numbers, topping sales figures everywhere. By early 1956 more than 299 Shand recordings had been issued and the chart listed *Bluebell Polka* sales as having passed the 100,000 mark.

Jimmy and the band made regular half hour broadcasts on the BBC Home Service in the Scottish Dance Music series and in April the Light Programme broadcast the Accordion Day Festival from London, featuring Jimmy and the celebrated Toralf Tollefson. On Saturday 12 May, Jimmy and the band really excelled themselves. They broadcast a radio programme at 6.55 p.m., and at 10.30 p.m. the same evening they were appearing in 'The Kilt is my Delight' – a television show compered by Ian Wallace, the popular actor and singer.

Up until that time an evening newspaper had been asking why Jimmy and the band had not appeared on television, and had suggested that something be done about it. Another paper speculated as to whether Jimmy would wear a kilt and concluded he probably wouldn't, as he would not want to be different from the band, his well-documented shyness having gone before him. The questions were answered in the first television performance when Jimmy *and* the band wore kilts. There they were seen by the viewing nation – kilted, sporraned, tartan-hosed and sporting frothy, lacy ruff fronts. The one exception to this uniform presentation was Jimmy, who felt that the lacy ruff was not for him and he wore his sober collar and tie!

The fine Fife tenor, James Urquhart, who was to appear in many television shows with Jimmy and the band, told David Phillips about what a harrowing experience the medium could be for artistes at that time.

> Performances were live, which was a big enough strain.
> Throw in a few technical hitches, which were not
> uncommon, and it only needed some last minute alteration

in the programme after everything seemed to have been ironed out, and you had all the makings of a state of rigid terror instead of conditions conducive to relaxed performance. But if Jimmy's 'attitude' to show business was that of the most reluctant amateur, his performance – and that of his band – was professional to an impressive degree. There were no idiot cards (visual prompting system) then; if a vocalist dried up, well that was just that.

The band never needed any musical prompting of course, never having had a scrap of music in front of them during any performance anywhere, even at the most lavish Highland Ball where they would be called upon to play for scores of dances. Nor were there any zoom lenses, which meant that the entire camera crept in on you for a close-up; at times I felt it was going to try and get right down my throat! It wasn't easy trying to warble away unconcernedly as the baleful glassy eye got nearer and nearer...

This new experience did not seem to hold any terrors for Jimmy and the band, as they produced a performance in their usual perfect tempo. There may have been a full scale war with butterflies inside, but the public face masked that. A journalist had persuaded Jimmy to promise to give a wee smile and one or two fans wrote to the newspapers later, claiming to have seen it.

Take it a bit easier! Jimmy had become almost a national hero and none of the 15,000 people who turned up for an open air concert in Aberdeen would disagree with that title. The traffic had been brought to a standstill and as Jimmy remembers, 'The floors were a wee bit damaged.' One person on whom that day made a lasting impression was a young Robbie Shepherd.

The *Daily Record* asked their readers to nominate 'Scotland's Number One Scottish Dance Band Leader' and announced the result a short while later with the headline 'SHAND'S THE MAN, you made him an easy first.' Jimmy was very pleased with the honour, but would have been just as happy if he had not won, as he liked and appreciated all Scottish dance bands. 'I ken maist o the leaders, an I like them a', an their styles,' he was quoted as saying.

The choicest plum in the teuchter players' calendar was handed to Jimmy and the band in 1956. They were asked to provide the music for the annual Gillies' Ball at Balmoral. Later, while appearing at the Albert Hall in London with Robert Wilson, Jimmy was practically mobbed by the audience of 7,000. After he left, or rather escaped, from London, he went on to play at Windsor Castle and then, ever matter-of-fact, he drove straight home.

Jim Ritchie had been playing the fiddle from a young age and won the 'strathspeys and reels' section for under sixteens at the Perth Musical Festival when he was twelve. With Jean Fairweather at the piano and Will Cameron, another fiddler, Jim played his first dance in Glenshee Hall when he was thirteen. By the time he was fourteen, Jim, with his box-playing pal Donald Ferrier, was entertaining audiences at concerts, raising funds for the Red Cross. They learned their tunes from Geordie's collection of Jimmy Shand records. Geordie's father ran the Glenisla Hotel, and when he booked Jimmy Shand to play at Glenisla School the boys could hardly believe it. 'Neither o's slept for a week beforehand,' Jim remembers. When the shy accordionist stepped in front of the audience, 'I felt the hair on the back o my neck fair risin an bristlin, an that's the Goad's truth!' he continued. He vowed there and then that some day he would play in a Shand band. He was working along with his parents on Wester Bleaton Farm when he first heard Jimmy and the band on the wireless. Although he was supposed to work at the ploughing until 5.30, he arranged with his mother to shout out of the window when Jimmy came on at 5.00. When he heard his mother's voice, he secured the horse's reins, vaulted the fence and reached the window in time to hear a matchless rendering of *Auchmountain's Bonnie Glen*. When the fiddle became his work, Jim played for the Hawthorn Band for four years.

He joined the Shand band in 1956 after playing fiddle for Bobby McLeod for five years. The McLeod band had been touring with Robert Wilson's White Heather Group, but the contract had nearly finished. Jim had given Bobby a month's notice, when Robert Wilson asked him, whilst they were in London, to stay on with the group as a soloist. The Shand band were also in London, making records, when Jimmy spoke to Jim. 'An are ye gaein wi Robert?' he asked. Jim said he really felt like having a rest as he had been very busy. Jimmy commented, 'Aye. Well, pity. I could've done wi ye...' Jim did not need to be asked twice and found himself busier than ever. Jim remembers the schedule just after he joined:

Talk aboot farm worker's days aince bein fae dawn tae dusk – my hours were not likelier tae be dawn tae dawn awa fae the farm! For ins'nce, I'd hae tae be awa fae Wester Bleaton in Glenshee by 6 a.m. tae meet the band bus at Perth at seeven, tae get tae the BBC at Glasgow by half past nine. We'd rehearse a' day for the show gaein oot at aroond half past six that nicht. Ah, but we were only startin! We'd be awa then tae play at a dance, maybe Lanark, until aboot twa in the mornin. It'd be six or seeven a.m. when I got back tae the glen. Except of coorse we'd been playin doon sooth, then it weel might be eleven next forenoon before I'd see the farm again. I've seen me gettin hame fae, say, London; gaein tae bed at midday, tae be up and awa again three hours later.

Oh, aye, since the band was in great deman a' place, there were local jobs now an then. Like the Kirkmichael Boolin Club. They wanted us for their annual dance, but it would hae tae be on a Friday tae ensure a guid turnoot. Well, Jimmy couldna gie them a Friday an my, ye've nae idea how dubious the committee was aboot the advisability o bookin any ither nicht! Speak aboot a prophet haein nae honour in his ain country! What a job I had persuadin them they could hardly lose wi Shand's band on whatever night. Finally, they kind o reluctantly agreed tae a Tuesday nicht – then nae sooner was this settled than we learned that another organisation had booked anither band for *their* dance on the Friday! Of coorse, the Bookin Committee need never have worried – a selloot; they were turnin fowk awa, had tae shut the doors.

A somewhat different local job was the Gillies' Ball at Balmoral. They got a fell good crowd there an a' incidentally. A richt swell affair. The band were up on a balcony at one end o the ballroom; at the ither end there was anither balcony where the Royal party would appear. Did they dance? Aye. The Queen Mother requested the *Dashing White Sergeant* and went through it gracefully wi her twa dochters. The same thing happened at Windsor Castle later on.

Take it a bit easier; Jimmy claims he reminded himself every now and then, in this his busiest year.

Following the tradition they had established more than ten years before, Jimmy and the band brought in the New Year on the radio for the BBC and then made their way back to 16 Sutherland Street to join the Hogmanay party. There seemed to be more people than ever before squeezed into the little living room – relatives and friends, fiddlers and sopranos, bass players and baritones, producers, radio and TV technicians, folk from next door and from far overseas, and box players of all shapes and sizes. There was, as always, plenty to eat and drink and more in reserve if needed. Erskine and David slept upstairs without a care in the world, while Anne was in her element coping marvellously with the situation. Toasts were offered and drunk: 'Here's tae a prosperous New Year'; and very enthusiastically, 'Here' s tae Jimmy Shand!'

Jimmy was 48 and more famous than he could ever have thought possible. If he had walked from his house in any direction he would not have gone far without hearing the sounds of his own virtuosity drifting out from behind some curtains or blinds. He was the host in his own home on this the most Scottish of all nights, but thanks to electronic communication he was the 'Guest of Honour' in millions of other homes. Jimmy remembered with affection the many happy New Years Anne and he had welcomed in their little semi-detached house in Sutherland Street and wondered what the future might bring.

In the 25 January 1957 edition of the *Radio Review*, a journalist found himself in a quandary.

As an innocent Sassenach, I asked an Aberdeen girl last week why Jimmy Shand always strikes me as having 'something' the other Scots band leaders haven't got.

'Is it something about his rhythm?' I said.

'Rhythm?' she said. 'It's more than that. Jimmy seems to catch a beat or emphasis that sets Scottish feet tapping, and hearts too. We love his absolutely strict tempo, which makes him so popular in Ireland as well as Scotland.'

Well, there you have it. I'm inclined to call this son of Dundee 'the Victor Sylvester of Caledonia', and if anyone quarrels with that description, have pity on a poor Sassenach!

Adopted son of Dundee, yes, but still a Fifer at heart!

Take it a bit easier. Of course, Jimmy had meant to heed this advice, but he hadn't and in March 1957 he wished he'd done so. He was sitting in his chair at home, all dressed up and ready to go, his evening suit under his overcoat, but he could not rise as his doctor was standing right over him. 'I'll be a' richt,' Jimmy said, but the doctor shook his head and said, 'I'll do a deal with you Jimmy. Temperature below 100 – off you go. Over 100 – off you go...to bed!' He had bronchitis, threatening pneumonia, and that put him out of action for three weeks.

Once he was back on his feet again Jimmy restarted the long journeys with the band but, this time it was different. He was honouring long-standing commitments but not accepting further work. The press soon got to hear about this arrangement and the *Daily Mail* published the headline: 'Retiring? Jimmy's far too young.' Anne was quoted as saying 'Jimmy retiring? Goodness me no! But he *is* gien up his playing for an indefinite period on medical advice.' The *Dundee Courier* broke the news at the end of April that Jimmy was, 'packing up at the peak of his career.' The paper went on to say that his last public appearance would be at the twice-yearly ball of the Manchester Caledonian Society. Jimmy was quoted at the time as saying, 'I've heard that I'm supposed tae be dyin, that I'm gaein intae hospital an that I'm retirin for good. I'm even supposed tae have collapsed behind the scenes when we played at the Palace Theatre recently. The truth is I've been workin too hard. I may be back; I dinna ken.'

The BBC had been aware of the situation for a while and had been pre-recording Jimmy and the band at Dundee's Coldside Studio to enable them to taper off their regular broadcasts. When asked at the time: 'What's going to happen to the band Jimmy?' he answered, 'I want them tae carry on withoot me; they can use my bus if they like. I'll supply letters o introduction tae organisers. A'body will say I should be awa on a cruise an a' that nonsense, but I'll enjoy myself just as much potterin aboot. It'll be a great relief tae ken I'm free.'

The press mournfully had a field day. The *Daily Record* produced the headline 'Jimmy Shand's Last Dance', followed by, 'Scotland's number one ambassador of music has quit'. 'Jimmy Shand Gives Up' was the banner heading in the *People's Journal*, but they had some extra information, 'And so do two of his band!' The newspaper reported:

> What of the band that has served him faithfully through the years? It has experienced shows without Punch before. The Shand Band went its merry music-making way while the maestro was in hospital for a stomach operation. It was the same when Jimmy toured America and Canada. The knights of King Jimmy absorbed so much of his rhythm that sometimes the dancers scarcely missed the king himself. But this time the outlook is not so bright. For the Jimmy Shand Band is not only losing Jimmy Shand. It is in fact being split in half. When the boss announced his decision, Syd Chalmers, violinist and one of the band's most skilled musicians, decided that he too would retire for the present. So did accordionist George McKelvey.

In July 1957, Jimmy and Anne made an announcement which surprised many of his friends and fans. They were leaving Dundee and moving to a substantial villa on a hill overlooking Auchtermuchty in Fife. The Sutherland Street semi was advertised for sale and Anne told reporters at the time, 'We'll be sorry to leave. We've made a lot of friends; on the other hand it'll be a lot easier for oor friends in Leven and Buckhaven tae visit us.' Jimmy admitted that he had always wanted to live in the country and looked forward, as he put it, 'tae get back tae the quiet life.'

He only appeared twice after his last official appearance on 26 April. The first occasion was for the children at the Baldovan Institution, and the other was with the band at the wedding of Ronald, the son of his pianist Norrie Whitelaw.

He received many messages, protests, condolences and dozens of requests for him to make a comeback. Among the more impassioned pleas were some from London agencies. Jimmy's response was, 'But I'm still under medical supervision, and I could never gae back intae the game as deep as before. If I'm ever tae gae back it'll hae tae be on a casual basis.'

One message, which he received over the radio, deeply touched him. It was from the staff of the Australian Mawson Station in the Antarctic. They said, 'We have elected you and your band, Musicians of the Year.'

The new house was quite an adventure for the Shands, as Jimmy recalls, 'The new hoose? A braw situation; ye can see for twenty miles tae the south, a healthy place. 'Muchty's aye been celebrated for its air.'

On the day the Shands announced they were moving, Jimmy flew out to Germany from Prestwick Airport, which encouraged some people to hope he might very well make a comeback. The Hohner company had invited him to be their guest at their centenary celebrations at Trossingen. They also presented him with a brand new accordion, small enough for David, when he arrived. He played on German television and appeared as a featured personality on many newsreels. On returning home he was one of the guests at the opening of the BBC's new Television Centre in Glasgow. The *Daily Herald* speculated: 'Maybe he hasn't hung up his accordion for good after all.'

As far as Jimmy was concerned, the move to Fife was the most important venture to be considered. He recalls the night the family moved to Braidleys (the name of the house). 'A

Jimmy Shand at Braidleys

helluva night o rain. An Anne wasn't in the happiest o moods on account o the way the hoose had been neglected. Maist o the rooms badly needin painted and papered. Well, we had a labrador dog then caed Shane, an immediately we arrived he vanished tae inspect his new surroundins. An he took an instant likin tae the place. He turned up later lickin aff his chops the blood o some o a dozen or so hens he'd done for at a neighbourin ferm! Cost me a few quid, that did.'

Jimmy was to spend a few more quid before Braidleys was up to standard. The property had stood unoccupied for over two years and had no gas or electricity. It had an irregular water supply which trickled from a hill tank through 600 yards of piping which certainly needed renewed. When he arrived Jimmy could hardly find the driveway, it was so overgrown with weeds and lupins.

The house had with it three cottages, two semi-detached bungalows, two garages, a number of sheds and outhouses, and was set in two acres of mostly wilderness. Jimmy had been aware of the property for years, as he recalls. 'Little did I think when I used tae come ower here for Forbes in the thirties that this place would ever be mine. I sellt an accordion tae Chae Nicoll, a farm worker bidin in ane o the cottages attached tae the hoose.'

One of the things Jimmy and Anne had considered before moving was the 'Muchty air, as David was showing disturbing signs of increasing chestiness. Erskine remained in digs in Dundee to be near his work and complete his apprenticeship.

Initially, Jimmy had to have power installed throughout the house, while local joiners were called in to fit new windows and a new back door. Jimmy himself helped strip the paper from every wall and scrape the paint from every inch of woodwork. He climbed the high extending ladder and, brandishing a paint brush, gradually turned the outside of Braidleys from a dirty grey to a sunny yellow. He also got involved in knocking down outside walls, laying new paths and steps and digging for an underground well in the garden.

The spell of manual labour did Jimmy the world of good. He looked bronzed and fit and was lighter in weight than he had been for years. He made plans to turn part of one of his bungalows into a studio and music room and also to set aside a small room off his dining room as an office.

One of the people who moved into one of Jimmy's cottages at Auchtermuchty was Andy Gow, the 'Bonnie Dundee' bus driver, who willingly helped to clear the land and lay paths.

In September, some newspapers published photographs of Jimmy working on his estate and when asked as to whether he would play again, he answered, 'I've some really good work fixed up for the future, but it's too early yet to say any more.'

Jimmy's friend, the journalist Alan Dunsmore, wrote a new batch of stories for the *People's Journal* dealing with the years since 1953. As before, the readers responded with numerous letters such as the following:

> Jimmy is president of our society, the Whitley Bay Country Dance Society, and often visits us here. Has anyone seen the band, including Jimmy, dance an eightsome reel as we have

done? We arrange for records to be played, and the band join us in quite a number of dances.

Mrs B. Lei, Hon. Secretary, Whitley Bay

At the close of last year's Edinburgh Festival Jimmy and his band were playing in Princes Street Gardens. Like many others about my age, 70, I couldn't resist dancing to that glorious rhythm. We old folk didn't mind who saw us whirling about and it was a 'reel' night out for all of us. When it was all over I heard some interesting tributes to Jimmy. His lively tunes had cured rheumatism, killed corns, taken headaches away, disposed of worries and made young again the oldest of the aged dancers!

A.B.M., Edinburgh

My husband started to sweep the chimney, but the brush stuck and nothing would budge it. I knew that neighbour Jimmy had a long ladder and that he'd been in the fire brigade. I called at his house to see if he could help, but he was out for the evening. Mrs Shand said she'd tell him when he came home. About ten o' clock we heard someone outside. It was Jimmy. He climbed to the roof and unstuck the brush. We thought that he would have waited 'til next morning, but though it was a dark winter night Jimmy came to our aid as soon as he heard about our spot of bother. No wonder he is such a popular man!

Mrs Taylor, Dundee

I worked beside Jimmy with the Fife Electric Company. Some time after he left us to go to Dundee a gang of us were laying a cable in Anstruther. We had just made tea one day when a car stopped and out got Jimmy. I asked him if he'd time to give us a tune... and he entertained us in great style. Then an old woman came to her door and threw a penny to him. In his quiet way he told her he was not playing for pennies. As he left us, the old woman followed him, a tear in her eye, because she had been so touched by his music and she handed him a big cigar.

Tom Allan, Cupar

At one time we lived with the Wards and their young son Allan at Branston Mains, Haddington. When we left to come and live in Dundee beside Jimmy Shand, we invited them to come and see us. Joe Ward is an ardent Shand fan, and he wondered if he'd see his idol when visiting us... Jimmy said, sure, bring him round. One evening we were setting off for a run to Glamis when we noticed Jimmy's car standing at his door. My husband thought this was a good chance to take Joe to meet the great man. Joe, Allan and my husband went to the door which I watched from the car. I saw them disappear inside and I waited – and waited – and waited! Apparently Jimmy had immediately picked up his accordion and said to Joe 'just say what ye'd like'. For an hour and a half he played to his delighted little audience. When they at last joined me in the car they looked as if they'd just inherited a fortune!

Mrs Brown, Carmylie

When Jimmy played at a dance in Dundee's Caird Hall, my wife's mother was close on 90, but she was determined to hear the maestro. We decided we'd let her watch from the balcony for half an hour, but once her feet got tapping she simply refused to leave. It was nearly half past eleven when we managed to coax her down the stairs. There we bumped into the man himself. In jest, he said to the old lady 'How's aboot a Broon's reel afore ye go?' She took him seriously and would have joined the dancers if we hadn't insisted we'd miss the last tram home.

When he was later playing in Marryat Hall, Dundee, I told him the old lady would like to come and hear him again. 'Let me know as soon as she arrives,' he said. I found he'd reserved a seat for her right at the front. When she said her favourite tunes were *The Bluebell Polka* and *The Duke and Duchess of Edinburgh* he made a last minute change in his programme and played them both. Afterwards he came over and spoke to her like a son. 'How's yer rheumatics?' he asked. She smiled and said, 'I havena felt a twinge a' night!'

Mrs James Jack, Dundee

There was also a letter from a young fan from halfway round the world:

Dear Mr Shand

I like your music very much so this is why I am writing to you. I like getting famous people's autograph so as you are so famous in New Zealand I would thought I would write and get your auto-graph. My mother and father are going to see you but I am not aloud to because I will be in the middle of my half yearly exams.

We got a lot of your records and I love Scottish music very much. Do you think I could please have your autograph. I know you are very busy but I hope you can. Thank you very much.

P.S. I have sent a stamped address envelope.

T.T., Wellington

By the end of October, the newspapers had something else to write about.

Nine

'It is my great privilege and pleasure to present the One and Only Jimmy Shand!' The words were from the celebrated ventriloquist Peter Brough, the time was 7.50 p.m., the venue, the Empire Theatre in Edinburgh, the date 21 October 1957. Jimmy Shand was back – back with a new box, a re-constituted band but still with the old magic. The theatre audience erupted into a crescendo of applause which swamped the familiar rhythm of *Bonnie Dundee*, the band's signature tune.

The buzz of excitement circulated the auditorium as one favourite tune followed another and all the while Jimmy stood stiff and erect with only his foot keeping time for his hands. They were still playing at 8.40 when the second house for the evening should have been in. This was the man who had said to Peter Brough shortly before the show started when asked how he was, 'I'll be fine pleased after the first house is past.'

At the end of the triumphant evening Jimmy and the band followed the usual routine: they went home. Accordionist Bert Shorthouse was dropped off in Dunfermline, bass fiddler Doug Maxwell at Seggieden and most of the others in Dundee. Fiddler Jim Ritchie even went back to his farm at Kirkmichael in Perthshire. Jimmy was always happy to turn into the driveway to Braidleys, as he said, 'There's nothing like gettin back tae yer ain bed.' After a week of packed houses Jimmy and the band moved on to the Glasgow Empire to conquer the audiences in the west.

Jimmy was back with a bang, but he was determined not to overdo things – he said. He certainly was happy about moving to Auchtermuchty as he felt he could relax there. When asked at the time how things were working out he said, 'The main reason for moving there was David's health. The fresh clean air has done him a world o guid. The bad cough he had in Dundee has gone, and he's as happy a lauddie as ye could meet. Auchtermuchty is central tae many areas o Scotland; and that's handy for a traivellin musician.'

The successes kept Jimmy and the band rolling along into the next year and initiated an unusual situation. Parlophone wanted to make some recordings, but Jimmy and the band had far too many commitments to be able to get to London at a time suitable to everyone. The solution Parlophone came up with was to go to Leeds where Jimmy and the band were booked to play at a university dance. Recordings were made during the dance and instead of a 'better than no recordings at all' situation, the resultant LP, *O'er the Border,* became a best seller. This was the first of Jimmy's LPs to include the innovative idea of giving the correct number of bars for each dance.

Arriving at a Fitchet family wedding reception, Jimmy found he was the only man wearing evening dress when the others had on lounge suits. He went home to change, but when he got back the meal was in progress so he sat down and composed *Betty Fitchet's Wedding,* an unusual but lasting present for the bride. Jimmy found that tunes 'sorta came tae him' on many occasions.

The Glasgow Alhambra was the venue for the 1958 Royal Command Scottish Variety Performance and Jimmy and the band got such a tremendous reception it led to a special comment the following day. On such an occasion the bill was composed of a wide range of outstanding acts, but Ian McFadyen, the BBC producer who had recorded the Command Performance, mentioned to Jimmy at an outside broadcast at Dalbeattie the next day that the greatest applause registered on their instruments had been for Jimmy and the band.

In December of the same year, the Royal Family were the audience again as they asked Jimmy and the band to play at Windsor Castle. After these engagements in the Royal castles or palaces, Jimmy and the band used to infuriate their wives, Anne included, by failing to remember what the Queen or the

Queen Mother was wearing.

1959 was another good year for the band and also for Jimmy as a solo performer. The British Accordion Federation conducted a poll and Jimmy was voted the Most Popular Accordionist in Great Britain.

Erskine in the meantime had finished his apprenticeship as a motor mechanic with Lamb's Garage in Dundee. Since his early teens he had filled in with Jimmy's band as a second accordion or pianist in emergencies; therefore it is not surprising he formed a little part-time group of his own, which built up its own worthy reputation. Erskine, who took one of his other names and called himself Jimmy Shand Jr., professionally, played the same music as his father but was not a copy-cat. Quite early on, when he was being tutored in the accordion, he opted for a different type of box. He preferred the 5-row Continental Chromatic to Jimmy's 3-row British Chromatic.

When Erskine moved to Braidleys he devoted himself to playing and working around the house. Work included months of digging to make room for a swimming pool. Work of a more musical but non-playing nature meant relieving Jimmy of many of the accordion repairs which had been sent or brought in by players from as far away as Ireland.

On the playing side, Jimmy Jr. teamed up with Robert Wilson on radio and TV, as well as touring round the country. Some of their engagements meant visiting Ireland and Germany.

1960 was as busy as Jimmy and the band wanted it to be, with live performances at various venues and broadcasting and recording work. The *Heather Mixture* shows for the BBC were extremely popular, due in no small part to the atmosphere created in the studio. Apart from Jimmy and band, the shows contained an extra ingredient from the second broadcast. On the first show Jimmy and the band performed to their celebrated standard, but the studio audience, who had been encouraged to dance, seemed reluctant and only a few couples out of 500 people took to the floor. Jimmy had the answer to this problem – he went to see Tom Elliot.

Jimmy had met Tom soon after the war and was very impressed by him and his enthusiasm for Scottish Country Dancing. Tom was an ex-champion gymnast, who believed in keeping himself fit by Scottish Country Dancing; or rather, as he said to the newspapers when he was 67, 'It's Jimmy Shand who's kept me fit, his music's like a medicine. When Jimmy's playing, I can dance 22 dances a night without feeling tired. I'm a physical drill man and I know the explanation. It's a question of timing. Some bands play just that little bit too slow, and for every moment you've to hang back a fraction of a second, that hanging back is tiring. Others may be a fraction fast and you tire just the same; Jimmy's music is a tireless music because its tempo is perfect.' From the second broadcast Tom was there – leading, involving and extorting. He cajoled the shy and instructed the doubtful. No excuse if the audience were unfamiliar with a dance, Tom was right in there demonstrating. He even said, 'If I thought things were going rather slowly I'd help to liven the party up with a few "hoochs".' By 1960 the *Heather Mixture* broadcasts were in the hundreds and Tom was still there aged 71, having missed only two shows.

Another series of live broadcasts in which Jimmy and the band were involved were the 'On Tour' shows. These programmes also involved other artistes and were broadcast from various parts of the country in front of audiences from the area. Jimmy had developed the marvellous talent of being able to compose tunes, and the programmes always opened with a tune specially composed for the town or district being visited. It was not uncommon for the band to be speeding towards a broadcast with Jimmy *de-diddle-de-di-ing* out the melody which they were expected to play without any mistakes a few hours later. Bert Shorthouse, who had joined the band as an accordionist, would take the air down in musical notation, but that was for future reference, as Jimmy and the band usually depended on their long-standing understanding when playing the tune.

115

James Urquhart, the tenor, recalled quite clearly a visit to Barra. After the show had been broadcast, Jimmy was asked to sit in with the local Castle Bay band at their Saturday night dance. From there James and Jimmy went to the headmaster's house, where they watched a showing of *Whisky Galore*, before going back to the hotel for a ceilidh. No hotel was going to be big enough to hold all the people who wanted to hear Jimmy play, and inevitably the ceilidh expanded out into the back by 3 a.m. The night was still not finished as Jimmy, in response to a request, made his way to a lonely cottage lit by a paraffin lamp. Here an old woman, who had been sitting by a peat fire, took great delight in welcoming Jimmy, James and her friends in. It was 6 a.m. before the night's entertainment was over and folk went home.

James Urquhart and Bert Shorthouse were the passengers in Jimmy's car when they sped northwards one day towards Forres for an 'On Tour' broadcast. Going at what Jimmy describes as a reasonable 90 mph, the car decided it did not want to go round a bend at the Forest of Bruar. It ploughed through the bushes and trees and came to a halt facing the river. James and Bert were somewhat shaken, and Jimmy discovered that a tree prevented him opening his door. A woman's voice asked, 'Are you all right?'

'Aye,' was Jimmy's reply.

'Are you sure?' the woman continued to enquire.

'Aye,' Jimmy said again and asked, 'could you contact the police?'

When a policeman arrived everyone was freed from the car and Jimmy was asked if he had been going fast. 'Na,' Jimmy said and explained why they had to get to Forres. Realising who they were, the policeman drove them to the nearest railway station and phoned ahead to Forres to let the BBC know what had happened. At Inverness station Andy Gow was waiting for them, having come along from Forres in the band bus. On reaching the hall they were due to broadcast from, Jimmy discovered he had left his box at Inverness railway station. Andy and Jimmy rushed back to Inverness and found that a porter had noticed the box and taken it into the office for safe-keeping. The broadcast went ahead to everyone's satisfaction but Jimmy remembers it was a long while before James Urquhart accepted a lift from him again.

In another incident involving a car going to an 'On Tour' broadcast, Jimmy's passengers were Anne and David. Jimmy was driving a hired car when he had to slow down behind a bus going through Old Scone. On a straight stretch of road outside of town, Jimmy overtook the bus and was hardly two car lengths in front when the car wobbled out of control and turned over. Anne lost her shoes and bruised her leg, while David was tossed around wondering what had happened. People came to their aid very quickly, including a doctor who had stopped by the roadside. After declining a lift to the hospital, Jimmy explained they needed to get to Kirriemuir for the broadcast. A phone call to Kirriemuir led to Andy Gow coming to pick them up in the band bus. After the broadcast the Shands were being driven home when the vehicle they were in mounted the bank on a bend. Luckily nobody was hurt, but David summed up all their feelings when he shouted from the back seat, 'Oh no! not again!'

In 1960 Jimmy went down to the Lyceum Ballroom in London and, before millions of television viewers, he was presented with his first Carl Alan Award, the 'Oscar' of the ballroom dancing world. The statuette of a dancing girl on a pedestal finished in gold was named after Carl L. Heiman and Alan B. Fairly, joint Chairmen of Mecca Limited. Jimmy was being recognised as the Most Outstanding Old Time Band Leader, which was a great honour of international standing. Also in 1960, Jimmy Jr. toured Australia and New Zealand with the Robert Wilson White Heather Group.

1961 started with what had now become a tradition for Jimmy and the band: bringing in the New Year on television; but the biggest party was still to come later in January when Jimmy and Anne celebrated their Silver Wedding. It certainly turned out to be that in more ways than one. Jimmy thought that the Queen's Hotel in Auchtermuchty would be the best place for their celebration, but the fact that the reception room could only hold 100 ruled it out. The venue was changed to the Auchtermuchty Victoria Hall and the invitations were sent out. Two days before the event Jimmy and Anne went down to plan the seating and discovered that with 240 acceptances to the reception this hall was also too small. Jimmy got into his car and quickly drove to the neighbouring village of Strathmiglo, which had a fine big public hall. Seeking out the hall committee chairman, the local schoolmaster Ian Inglis, Jimmy pleaded, 'Can I have the hall for Wednesday night?' The chilling answer was that the hall was already booked but...

Jimmy had raised hundreds of pounds for the hall funds, for the old folks and for the proposed Strathmiglo 'Meals on Wheels' service. The village did not forget this and decided to put him first. The previously scheduled public meeting was moved to the annexe and Jimmy and Anne's party was allocated the main hall.

For the next two days Jimmy spent a lot of time phoning and driving over three counties to inform their guests about the change of plan. On the evening itself, over 90 cars arrived in Strathmiglo carrying guests for the party. Nine waitresses were rushed off their feet manoeuvring through the packed hall, serving boiled ham and steak pie, and Jimmy was greeted with a great cheer when he said, 'Drink what ye like – it's a' on the hoose the nicht!'

The three-tier Silver wedding cake weighed 35 lbs and was adorned with tartan ribbons and white heather decorations, as well as a cut-out standing figure of Jimmy in Highland dress holding an accordion. The baker was Alex Fraser, who had provided their wedding cake 25 years before. Mr Fraser was enough of a canny businessman to display the cake in his shop window the week preceding the celebrations!

Among the congratulatory telegrams read out was one from

Jimmy and Anne's Silver Wedding
(© Alex G. Cowper)

ventriloquist Peter Brough and another from his equally famous dummy, Archie, which read 'Lang may yer lum reek – Woodenhead Andrews.' Bobby Watson, the dancer, and his wife Mavis, sent a telegram from Aberdeen saying, 'You have pedalled uphill for 25 years – may you reach the 50 without changing gear.' Andy Gow placed a large box on Owney McCabe's head and pointed him in the direction of the top table. The box contained a silver tea and coffee service and the message, 'From the Bandie and Andy to Shandy'.

The Rev Thomas Lithgow, the local minister, said a few words including, 'It is a very big occasion in two lives when two people undertake a very solemn promise, and it is gratifying to see two people who have kept that promise and kept it so well.'

Jimmy and Anne led off the dancing with an old fashioned waltz, Anne resplendent in a silk costume in two shades of blue and Jimmy making a colourful impact wearing a brown suit and a green shirt. Between dances he had a chance to catch up with old friends and have a blether. There was Mrs Margaret McNab from Leven, who had played the piano for Jimmy in the 1930s, Dr Sandy Tulloch, Jimmy's long-standing confidant and fellow box player, and Tom Elliot who although 71, still led off the dancing in all Jimmy's *Heather Mixture* radio broadcasts. Also in the company was Mrs Denham, Jimmy's landlady when he first moved to Dundee.

Jimmy's brother John and Anne's niece Joan, the best man and bridesmaid twenty five years before, helped keep the crack going and it was remarked by some that they hadn't seen Jimmy smile so much for many a day. Jimmy and Anne relaxed and were happy among their ain folk; and Jimmy himself, when he was not dancing, could listen for a change to his own kind of music played by Ian Arnott. Jimmy's comments on being overwhelmed by the numbers and the warm reception were, 'Next time it'll hae tae be the Kirkcaldy Ice Rink.'

By 1961 Jim Ritchie decided he *did* need a rest from the wearingly hectic life and retired from the band. The fact that he lived in Glenshee sometimes added to his problems as far as travelling was concerned. His car occasionally broke down in the middle of nowhere in the middle of the night, and in winter his home was inaccessible at times under heavy falls of snow. He had to lodge with the Shands for a week at one time as he could not get home. Jim decided to freelance and fill his time learning to play the bagpipes, throw the hammer, put the shot, fish and compose. Sleep was given a high priority as was listening to Jimmy Shand records. Syd Chalmers returned to the band to take the fiddler's seat.

On 2 April, Jimmy, George McKelvey and Bert Shorthouse joined Kenneth McKellar, Alex Finlay, Lucille Graham, Bobby Watson and Denis Woolford on a tour of Australia and New Zealand. This had been arranged after Jimmy had spoken to promoter George Mennie, when he was home on holiday in Aberdeen.

The Scots' route took them via Italy to land at Darwin. From there they flew to Brisbane for the first Australian engagement. George McKelvey was the pianist for the band on the tour while Bert Shorthouse's piano accordion supported Jimmy's button accordion. Bass players were engaged locally as the tour went along.

Jimmy's music was already well known and very popular Down Under, and in one case to a very novel extent. The souvenir programme for the tour included the following statement – 'Popular Jimmy Shand's breezy accordion music has won him the title of "Pied Piper of Philip Island".' Philip Island is one of Victoria's tourist resorts famous for its penguins. The programme notes continued, 'Round about eight o'clock of an evening, when the tourists are mustered by the shore, the music of Jimmy Shand is played over the waters and the penguins come marching in, firstly single file, then in columns of twos and threes.' After reading this Jimmy knew he was assured of at least one audience and a well dressed one at that!

There were many welcoming letters waiting for Jimmy including the following unusual one:

> We are thrilled to have you all with us; we have been waiting for a long time for such a visit from world class Scottish artistes... my name is Pat Lee, a past member of the Australian Antarctic South Pole Expedition of 1957; we sent you a message from

Mawson Base choosing you the musician of the year. My
cobber, Sandy Sandilands met you while he was in Scotland...
we would like to meet you after the show if at all possible... if
any of your party would like a run down the South coast, Bulli
Pass, Woolongong, Shell Harbour... the tie-pin is from the
South Pole and is one of Captain Scott's pony nails used during
1909–1912 fatal journey. While I was with Sir Edmund Hilary I
got the nail from Scott's old hut.

The Scots got a wonderful reception wherever they went,
playing to packed theatres and halls, being welcomed
everywhere by great crowds, pipe bands and dignitaries,
including mayors.

In Sydney they performed on an unusual stage – it revolved
slowly – which prompted Kenneth McKellar to compare it to
playing in a gent's outfitter's window. Good newspaper
reviews followed each of their performances, one of which in
Melbourne must have pleased a certain Scottish tenor: 'Kenneth
McKellar, surely one of the finest tenors Melbourne has had the
good fortune to hear, held the audience spellbound...' George
McKelvey met up with his younger brother James and his
family, and stayed with them in their Melbourne home instead
of the group's hotel. George introduced James to Dickie
Murray, the leader of the Melbourne Country Dance Band and
James was asked to play with them on many occasions. After
three weeks, the tour party moved on to New Zealand.

The visit to New Zealand gave Jimmy the chance to have a
reunion with some long-lost relatives, particularly an uncle and
his family who had emigrated when Jimmy was four years old.
As in Australia, all the artistes received lavish praise in the
press; and in each city and hall they played in, a pipe band
paraded before them to introduce the programme. An
Auckland newspaper commented: 'Alex Finlay, a comedian,
whose mere appearance on the stage was enough to make the
audience laugh and whose humour kept them convulsed...
This show is undoubtedly one of the best of its type seen in
Auckland. It has everything a good show needs.' Later in the
tour a press notice said, 'One of the best musicals to visit
Palmerston North... right down the list of artistes it was a show

122

packed with entertainment.' Bobby Watson came in for particular praise for 'his amazing lightfootedness and novelty interpretations of familiar dances.' A highlight of Bobby's act was playing the bagpipes while dancing.

At Palmerston North Jimmy renewed an auld acquaintance with Jock Thompson, whom he had last seen 37 years before in Fife. Jimmy, when he was a young pit boy, used to sit near the band in which Jock played the box, just to listen and learn.

When the tour party stepped off the plane into the bright sunshine at Taieri Airport, they were met by a pipe band playing *Scotland the Brave* as a welcome to Dunedin. The people in this city, which regards itself as New Zealand's most Scottish city, certainly seemed to enjoy the two concerts at the Town Hall and the local newspaper reported that the audience, 'gave an excited welcome unequalled for a group of entertainers since Sir Harry Lauder was here more than thirty years ago.'

The group's next appearance was in Invercargill, after which they flew home via San Francisco. After all the excitement what did Jimmy do? 'We just carried on the same as before, full diaries, here there an everywhere.'

Later in the year Jimmy had to set aside some time to travel to London to pick up his second Carl Alan Award.

Jimmy's record three Carl Alan Awards, 1960, 1961, 1962

Ten

Jimmy was not impressed by what he saw when he looked in the mirror at his house in March 1962. 'Noo, be honest Anne – dae ye no think it's a wee bit...' Jimmy remembers saying, his voice tapering away.

'A wee bit nothing! It suits ye just grand. What else would ye wear? A' the men'll be dressed the same, ye wouldna like tae stand oot different, shairly?' Anne said.

Jimmy and Anne outside Buckingham Palace after his MBE presentation

Jimmy's difficulty was he felt uneasy in the clothes he was wearing. They were not some new outlandish sixties fashion with flower patterns and beads, but the most snobbish of English attire – morning dress. Perhaps he could thole the trousers, jacket and tie but the problem was the grey lum hat. He was convinced he had been conned into wearing the tallest ever made!

He recalls saying, 'Tell ye one thing, Anne, it's a guid joab there's nae sna aboot – I wouldna dare appear in the streets, jist be a proper invitation tae lauddies wi sna bas a' place!' The reason he was even considering wearing the unfamiliar outfit was that he had been advised it was the correct thing to do when invited to drop in on the Queen at Buckingham Palace. When he took his leave of Her Majesty and the Duke of Edinburgh, he had a broad smile on his face and an MBE in his hand. The honour had been awarded for Jimmy's outstanding contribution to Scottish Country Dance Music. Anne was smiling as well, as she had been able to see for herself what the Queen wore for the occasion, and did not have to rely on, 'I dinna ken' or 'I think it might hae been a blue dress... couldna be sure though.'

Summer meant another trip, this time a longer tour of Australia and New Zealand than the previous year. Jimmy's 'band' this time consisted of George McKelvey, piano accordion, Syd Chalmers, fiddle, and Jim Scott on the piano. The lead tenor was Kenneth McKellar, again with his accompanist Denis Woolford. Among the newcomers were Moira Anderson, Duncan Macrae, and Jimmy Warren as comic and compere.

Duncan Macrae was already well known, as many of his films such as *Whisky Galore* and *Tunes of Glory* had been seen all over the world. His contribution to this tour, however, was as a comic monologist, and his fame had gone before him due to a certain *Wee Cock Sparra* poem. When he performed it, complete with flying limbs and facial expressions, he brought the house down everywhere they went. One critic, referring to his performance in the St James Theatre in Auckland, wrote that it had been worth waiting a long time to see him exhibit his physique – stripped to a kilt of alarming brevity and very little else, 'resembling an over-grown string bean.' In other papers his 'undertaker' skit was praised for his being able to make 'a ghoulish topic funny, but not offensive.' 'Hysterically funny' was how the newspapers in Hawke's Bay described his performance!

The 'Little Breath of Scotland' that Kenneth McKellar promised to audiences was hailed in Wellington as a show which hit with a gale force. The review of the show at the Embassy Theatre in Hamilton referred to Moira Anderson's performance in the following manner: 'Few could restrain their tears when stage lights were dimmed and her haunting voice implored *Come Back to Bonnie Scotland.*' Moira and Kenneth got rave reviews everywhere, especially when they decided to discard their microphones and moved closer to the audience.

The *Border Watch* newspaper reported: 'A joyousness running through the entire programme due to the way the artistes put their hearts into their performances, a labour of love obviously, which quickly established a rapport with the capacity audience… well worth seeing – and taking part in.'

The *Palmerston Times* came straight to the point with its headline: 'Hoots Mon! – What a Grand Nicht'.

The *Dunedin Evening Star* mentioned the three thousand people who had packed the main Town Hall and also wrote, 'There can be few touring shows capable of drawing such a crowd.' Praise was also given to Denis Woolford for his piano solos, and Jimmy Warren's material was welcomed as being free from smut.

Jimmy and the band had the audiences lilting and tapping – and in many cases stamping – their feet all over Australia and New Zealand for seven weeks, but so far as the radio listeners in Scotland were concerned, they had never been away. The BBC had pre-recorded a batch of *Heather Mixture* shows and were broadcasting them at their regular times.

Anne in Auchtermuchty listened to the broadcasts, and wrote in one of her letters that she was sure she had heard

Jimmy singing *cam-a-ree, cam-a-ro* in one of the programmes. Writing was the best way to communicate as the telephone service was very unreliable. Other letters mentioned how the swimming pool at the front of Braidleys had been fitted, and that a lean-to had been constructed beside the garage. Anne wrote that Jimmy's Aunt Rachel, who now lived with them, had not been well, but Erskine had taken her in the car to see old friends. Better news was that David was happy at the occupational centre at Cupar. Anne also mentioned that Ben Lyons, their BBC producer friend, was anxious to know if the rumours that the tour was going to be extended were true. As a postscript, she said she was glad to learn 'that the horse had won'.

Horse? What horse? An article in the *New Zealand Sporting Press* explains: 'Jimmy May Give Inspired Performance' ran the headline. 'One horse who may be capable of an inspired performance at Wangani this week is the Hawera four year old, Jimmy Shand, a candidate for the Waihou Maiden Race. The star item in Wanganui this week has been the visit of a team of Scottish troupers, including Jimmy Shand and his Band. So far the Blue Coral gelding has achieved nothing like the fame of his musical namesake, but he does have the recommendation of a promising fourth after a slow start in his last appearance.'

Jimmy Shand (the horse that is) won the mile race by 2½ lengths, in a field of thirteen at odds of £5 7s 6d: £1.00. Naturally Jimmy backed it and won £37.00.

When Jimmy returned home he was pleasantly surprised at the decorating work on the house done by Erskine. He was also impressed by Erskine's new records recorded as 'Jimmy Shand Jr.' and pleased that Andy Gow had been looking after the bus, the cars, the motor boat and motorbikes.

Jimmy's diary was quite full for the rest of the year, and included a visit to London to pick up the Carl Alan Award for the third year in succession. At the awards ceremony, Jimmy always met many important people in the music business and renewed old acquaintances, but in 1962 he was introduced to four newcomers from Liverpool who had been recording with George Martin, one of Jimmy's producers. Their names were John, Paul, George and Ringo, universally known as The Beatles. Jimmy also met Cilla Black in George Martin's office in Baker Street.

1963 was as busy as ever all over the country with Jimmy and the band fulfilling engagements and broadcasting commitments. Every now and then a newspaper or magazine would include an article or news item about Jimmy, but in March 1964 a more substantial feature written by David Phillips appeared in the *Scots Magazine*. This was a short review of Jimmy's life written from David Phillips' vantage point of being not only a writer friend but George McKelvey's cousin.

Just after publication of the feature, Jimmy set off on his third tour Down Under, again with Kenneth McKellar, Moira Anderson and Denis Woolford. The laughs this time were provided by the veteran Scottish comedian Jack Radcliffe, making his first trip; as were singers Robin Hall and Jimmy McGregor, who had more than 500 appearances on British television to their credit.

The tour programme notes stated: 'Shy Jimmy, the World at his Feet' (perhaps it should have been at his fingertips!), and went on to say, 'Never has the entertainment world seen anyone like Jimmy Shand, a balding 56 with a tiny, tidy, light toothbrush moustache, and an equally tiny public smile. He is uncompromisingly honest... a phenomenon of simplicity in a world of masks and false attitudes. When an audience sees Jimmy Shand on the stage, they are looking not only at Scotland's ace accordionist, but at the man himself.' This third tour lasting eleven weeks was a longer, equally triumphant series of appearances, when auld acquaintances were renewed. Anne's airmails kept Jimmy informed of Erskine's and David's doings, about who came to tea and what was going on in Auchtermuchty and round about.

In 1964 there were more than 120 registered pipe bands in New Zealand. At Invercargill the troupe was welcomed at the airport by the City of Invercargill Caledonian Pipe Band, playing a composition of Jimmy's, *Angus M'Leod of Achgrave*. When he learned from the Band President, Peter Anderson, that they had no signature tune, Jimmy promised to write them one, which he did in a matter of minutes on a Sunday outing a few days later. Delighted with the *City of Invercargill Caledonian Pipe Band March* the band had the original copy framed and gave it a place of honour on one of the bandroom walls.

It was in New Zealand that Jimmy saw The Beatles for the second time. They arrived in Wellington on the plane that the Scot's touring party were due to go out on. Jimmy remarked at the time, 'I think they are fine lauddies; guid luck to them. Some o these young groups can certainly put a number across... I'd like beat music a bit better if it wasna quite sae noisy.'

When he arrived back in Scotland near the end of July, Jimmy found himself fending off rumours that he planned to retire soon. Jimmy remembers his words at the time, 'Nae actual plans for retirement, but ye micht say I'm at something o a crossroads, and as far as dance dates are concerned I aim tae keep the diary a lot lichter fae now on. Mind, it's difficult, since I'm sae often refusing customers that have become auld freens, but, let's say ye lose yer keenness the aulder ye get...'

Jimmy was now 56, and he had a drummer and a second accordionist in the band who were older than he was. Despite this, there was still an insatiable demand for their services which had steadily increased over the years. A decision was made that perhaps the three of them at least should begin to take things a bit easier.

Well, at last they did. Much of the nocturnal speeding around the landscape – from village hall to castle, from theatre to club – was cut down, or rather not permitted to recur through only accepting more spaced-out bookings. So Jimmy now had more free time – which he made good use of, playing at hospitals, for old folk and for various charities. He also had more time to do things at home as well. He purchased his own cement mixer, which certainly did not mean doing away with all the garden and lawns, since he arranged to have carted in 15,000 tons of soil to build up one particular corner of his grounds to construct a putting green. He also planned to heat the water in the swimming pool.

He now had a bit more time to try out his speed boat on the River Tay, and had converted one of his sailing boats into a cabin cruiser leisure craft. His first love, so far as speed was concerned, was still motorbikes, and as he had several of these in his garages, he felt it only right that they should be taken in turns for a spin round the countryside.

Some people had written to the newspapers suggesting that the craze for beat music had swamped the interest in Scottish dance music and this had forced Jimmy to retire. Jimmy laughed when he read this, as it had been his own choice to do less work, but some country dance bands were not as busy as they would have liked to have been.

Jimmy Shand and his boat

In September 1964 Jimmy's old friend and fellow trouper, tenor Robert Wilson, died at his home in Ayr. He had been involved in a motoring accident earlier in the year and had never got over it. A year older than Jimmy, Robert had retired in 1962, still celebrated as the 'Voice of Scotland' after 32 professional years which started with the Rothesay Entertainers. Then he sang with the D'Oyly Carte opera company before launching out on his own as a concert singer. Obituaries spoke of his great success 'Down in the Glen', and how he had bridged the gap between Harry Lauder, Kenneth McKellar and Andy Stewart.

In 1965 Jimmy responded to more newspaper speculation about the fate of Scottish dance bands. One newspaper published the headline, 'Jimmy denies dance band blues'. 'Just rubbish!' was his comment when he was asked if the stories were true.

The fact that Erskine – as Jimmy Shand Jr. – had decided to disband his group, led Jimmy to deny the rumour that it was because of lack of engagements, due to the competition from beat music. His statement said, 'They are disbandin, true enough; but no through lack o work. It's just that he's choosin tae concentrate on runnin an accordion repair business full time. Full-time travellin aboot tae play is tough enough – but it's a lot harder when ye are only part time an trying tae keep abreast o ither work day by day, and, intae the bargain, he's plannin tae get married in the near future. Tae say that a' the public wants now is beat is tae talk pure nonsense. I still get mair offers o work than I can possibly accept – even if I was keen enough tae want tae fit it a' in.'

Erskine did get married to Margaret, a lass from Brechin, and they happily set up house in a farm cottage.

If there was any perceived or imagined lack of interest in Scottish music in Britain, the same certainly could not be said in Ireland. Jimmy's Irish fans had remained as true to him as he had to them. He had not only appeared in the Emerald Isle in public performances but also at private functions. The celebrated Irish accordionist and ceilidh band leader, Donald Ring, commented at the time, of the tingling blend of excitement and reverence with which fellow instrumentalists regarded Jimmy. 'Sure, he was a god to us, a god entirely. Ye see there's accordion players that have a good right hand; with others it is the left hand. Ah, but with Jimmy Shand it is both hands! There never was his like, nor is there likely to be again.'

Jimmy and the band continued on a more leisurely schedule, but even this was beginning to take its toll on Owney. He was determined he was not going to let Jimmy down but it was becoming obvious that he was struggling, not with his drumming, but with the travelling. Eventually Jimmy took him aside and after a great deal of sympathetic persuasion convinced him to retire. Owney's 'dunt' and Jimmy's time-keeping foot had maintained an effortless synchronisation of rhythm for the band for twenty five years.

The longest serving member of the band was now George McKelvey, but when details were being discussed about another tour of Australia and New Zealand the following year, he indicated he would gladly step down to enable another piano accordionist to make the trip. R.W. Lean, the tour promoter, on a visit to Scotland to sign up the band and the other artistes, was very impressed at the way Jimmy managed to get around Britain very quickly. Mr Lean wrote in his diary: 'When I arrived in London he had driven from Scotland to London Airport to greet me, and then drove back the next day to Scotland. It was mid winter, but he drove from Stranraer, where he had been appearing, and then on to Auchtermuchty where we arrived about four o'clock in the morning.'

The Shand Band for the 1966 tour consisted of Jim Johnstone on the piano accordion, Angus Fitchet with his fiddle, and Peter Straughan on piano. Other members of the troupe included vocalist Ivy Carey, baritone Ian McLeish and comedian Jimmy Fletcher. Having featured with the Shand band several times over the years, Jimmy Fletcher was hired for the tour at Jimmy's special request.

The Scots got a wonderfully warm welcome wherever they

went. The New Zealand *Taranaki Herald* greeted a new record by the band, *Step We Gaily*, with: 'Scotland's greatest export since whisky. There's a special lift of the heart that you get from Shand's product, something elusive and almost indefinable; but it's highly habit-forming and the charm of it is – there's no hangover.'

The tour continued to be a success which everyone enjoyed; both from the performing point of view and, judging by the reaction at the various venues, from the audiences' – but it was always good to get back home. At the same time Ian Powrie, the very successful Scottish Country Dance band leader, was settling his business and family affairs in Scotland and planning to live in Australia with his wife and two children. Ian was the fiddler son of the illustrious box player Will Powrie, who had had records on the market before Jimmy in the 1930s. He was also the same Will Powrie that Jimmy competed against at Alyth in 1933.

Earlier in the year, Ian had been on a tour of Australia with Andy Stewart, and had been offered a very attractive business opportunity. This, and the certainty of being able to see more of his family, helped him to decide on the move to Australia; it was not through lack of engagements in Scotland. His band was taken over by accordionist Jimmy Blue, who renamed it Jimmy Blue's Scottish Country Dance Band.

Although a younger musician than Jimmy, Ian had been finding that to enable him to have more time with his family he needed to taper off his commitments and this was proving to be very difficult. As he stated at the time, 'When your life revolves around the signing of contracts for everything – television, theatres, etc. – you have to honour these dates. It was impossible for me to taper away the band business. Limit the appearances and you are liable to get 'you played for them – why cannot you play for us?' and so it builds up again.'

Now that Jimmy was back in Scotland he still had the problems of manipulating his time in such a way as to give the band and himself an easier routine. In November 1966 he suffered from another form of manipulation, or rather lack of it. For a while he had been bothered with pain in his shoulder, and despite his best efforts, it could not be shrugged off; indeed there were times when he could not sleep because of the intensity of the pain. If things became intolerably uncomfortable, Erskine would fill in on some engagements, but Jimmy was loathe to admit he personally couldn't cope. A suggestion that a manipulative operation under anaesthetic would solve his problems proved to be unfounded, and the pain continued.

For the best part of seven months, he travelled from Auchtermuchty to Bridge of Earn Hospital each morning for treatment and exercises, but by the middle of August there was no discernible improvement and he couldn't play at all. To enable the band to fulfil its commitments, Erskine (as Jimmy Shand Jr.) was playing full-time.

Another problem was looming on the horizon, involving a commitment that Jimmy had made earlier. Jimmy Logan was going on a two-month tour of Canada and the US, starting in early September – and Jimmy was booked to go with him. He did go, and in some miraculous way he played. According to the newspaper comments during the tour, he managed to acquit himself more ambitiously than just the odd restrained vamp. The *Hamilton Spectator* had the headline 'Hoot Man It Swings' and went on to describe Jimmy as the 'Accordionist Supreme'. The same newspaper talked about him as 'having fingers spidering over the stops of the difficult instrument squeezing out toe-tapping music'. The reception at Winnipeg's Playhouse Theatre, according to newspaper reports, 'lapsed into a huge family gathering as though the audience, Logan and his five colleagues, shared some great secret. Perhaps Jimmy Shand... captured the secret best. Airs like *Loch Lomond,* the *Gentle Maiden, Afton Waters* and *Comin Through the Rye* trickled from his fingers on the button key accordion. As they did, the dead pan musician was surrounded by a sea of humming. The quickened pace of Highland pipers' dance tunes like *A Wee Drap O Scotch* brought almost universal toe-tapping and clapping. Shand managed his first smile in acknowledgement of applause at the curtain call.'

Jimmy Logan's five colleagues referred to in the newspaper article were vocalist Ivy Carey, the bearded bass baritone Bill McCue, the pianist John Crawford, and Ronnie Dale, who was talented on several musical instruments, as well as acting as second comic to Jimmy Logan and MC for the performances. The fifth person was Jimmy Shand himself, of course.

The *Vancouver Sun* had an unusual impression of Scotland and Scotsmen, as can be judged from the following report: 'Jimmy Shand has been entertaining Scotsmen almost as long as the Loch Ness monster. He has the stern aspect of a Presbyterian minister presenting the Scottish Football Cup to Glasgow Celtic, but he drew some warm and friendly sounds from his accordion – the only accordion I've heard with a Scottish accent.'

There were twelve cities on the United States part of the tour including Los Angeles, Pittsburgh and San Francisco. The official programme in San Francisco had an advertisement for the Edinburgh Castle Tavern, which promised bagpipes on Fridays and Saturdays, and a fish and chip shop which recommended, 'Eat with us or take it home in a Newspaper'. When Jimmy played the Carnegie Hall in New York there wasn't an empty seat in the house, with many more people waiting outside. He took the opportunity of this stay in New York to visit Jack Dempsey's Broadway restaurant, where he met the former heavyweight champion of the world and swapped autographs, not punches.

In 1968 Erskine and Margaret had a house built just across the road from Braidleys and moved in there with their daughter Diane. Erskine, as Jimmy Jr., appeared with Jimmy's band when they topped the bill for a fortnight at the Gaiety Theatre, Ayr, in May. This was the year that George McKelvey decided to retire after 25 years as second twiddle to take up a job as a car park attendant at a site down by the docks in Dundee. Many musicians dropped in to see him, which meant he kept up with what was going on, but he was still glad to get back to his own bed every night.

Norrie Whitelaw also retired, with his wife, to their flat in Caird Avenue, opposite the BBC's Dundee Coldside Studios. Later in the year, Erskine launched the Jimmy Shand Jr. five-piece band full-time, and took on engagements from Hammersmith Palais to the Scottish islands, and many one-night stands in between. They were also kept busy with recording dates and radio and television work.

In December 1968, a newspaper report was published referring to Jimmy playing for friends in Glenclova on New Year's Day. It said that the music had been provided by, 'what is perhaps the best known brand of music in the world, that of Jimmy Shand and his Band.' His band for that occasion was Angus Fitchet on fiddle, Peter Straughan on piano, and Ian Wilson on drums. Sometimes Bert Shorthouse supported on the accordion, at other times it was Jimmy Jr. Jimmy was taking care, or so he thought, not to let the pressures build up on him the way he had done before, but despite these precautions he collapsed in the late spring of 1970, suffering from exhaustion. By November he was off to London with the band for 'This is Scotland's Show', but he did not stay with them for the full English tour. The fact that care must be taken with his health was reinforced in his own mind by the death of Owney McCabe, his faithful drummer and very good friend, who had been with Jimmy since before the start of his professional career.

Jimmy bounced back again in 1971, taking on selected engagements as well as being invited to the mammoth star-studded BBC Variety Show which was staged in His Majesty's Theatre in Aberdeen in June. The bill included Moira Anderson, Jimmy Logan, Rikki Fulton, Jack Milroy, Lena Martel, Kenneth McKellar, Ian Wallace, John Grieve, Chic Murray, The Corries and many more. Jimmy was also committed to another series of *Heather Mixture* radio broadcasts, and although he had an occasional break, it seemed as if these would go on indefinitely. In March 1972 things did have to go on without him, as he collapsed again. The remaining programmes in the series were completed by Jimmy Jr. and Jim McLeod. The message was eventually getting through to Jimmy. The cutting down, the tapering off, was not working. The only thing that was going to work for him was not to work; therefore in 1972 he finally decided to retire, professionally that is. Retiring meant he now had more time to play in hospitals, or play for the old folks (many of whom were younger than he was!) and there were frequent occasions when many of his friends dropped in to Auchtermuchty for a chat and a tune.

Erskine was keeping the family traditions going, but was beginning to have trouble with two fingers of his right hand. It wasn't as if they were stiff or painful, it was just that the power seemed to be leaking away. He tried a range of treatments – including acupuncture, manipulative therapy and full voltage electrical stimulation – but to no avail.

In 1973 Jimmy may have retired, but he certainly wasn't forgotten, as many people still called upon him to play for many functions and charities. One of his great admirers and former band members, Jim Ritchie, proved himself to be a poet as well as a master fiddler, and wrote the following verses:

> Burns wrote hoo Niel Gow fiddled
> An hoo his elbow jinked an diddled,
> But a word or twa I'm sure he'd say
> Aboot the maestro o the present day.
>
> Born in Wemyss on the shores o Fife
> Whaur first he glimpsed the dawn o life,
> His humble parents then little thought
> What gift that day auld Scotland got...
>
> When at school an jist a laddie
> A melodeon he got fae his daddy;
> Wi genius art oot ower the keys
> He rattled oot the doh ray me's.
>
> 'Aye, gifted,' said the fowk a' roon
> When asked tae play a spree in the toon;

Father an mither were oh sae prood
But Jim was shy at thought o a crood.

Wi tremlin hand an blushin face
An box straps on his shithers placed –
Then! Hornpipes, jigs, strathspey an reel;
The place did shak wi toe an heel!

An some did stare engrossed in wonder,
Ithers roared applause like peals o thunder;
Until mair tunes o marchin beat
Took ilka dowp fae aff its seat.

An anes wha'd bickered quit their quarrel,
Louped an sang, an tasted the barrel;
Efter dancin in ane anither's erms
Gaed hame that nicht on better terms.

Far an wide at mill an merkit
Even city gents that sat an clerkit –
In ilka mind the same was planned;
'We'll hae a dance wi Jimmy Shand.'

In the fifties he took his toll
An won yon Public Opeenion Poll;
Carl Alan Awards twa or three;
On tap o that the MBE!

He plays wi sic art, ease an grace,
His playin ye'll tell like a weel-kent face;
I've danced tae many a different band
But nane comes near auld Jimmy Shand!

Jimmy's professional public performances may have finished,
but the music continued.

Eleven

The Jimmy Shand Story was the name given to the double album produced in 1973, in conjunction with Bryce Laing, Jimmy's record producer since 1968. It included tracks of music from various stages in Jimmy's career, but was not meant to be his final album. In the same year, Erskine finally had to give up playing professionally and opened a shop in Auchtermuchty selling, advising on, and sometimes repairing musical instruments. On 27 April of the following year, the Provost, Magistrates and Councillors of the Royal Burgh of Auchtermuchty conferred the Freedom of the Burgh on James Shand MBE, in recognition of his outstanding service to Scottish Country Dance Music and the community. Also in 1974, Ian Powrie, a long time friend, while on a visit home from Perth, Australia, got together with Jimmy at Craighall Studios in Edinburgh to make a long playing record with the appropriate title *When Auld Friends Meet*. The supporting musicians on the record were: Pam Brough on piano, Dave Barclay on bass and Arthur Easson on drums.

If a newspaper mentioned, or a poster promoted, a garden fête or a sale of work 'to be opened by Jimmy Shand' the event was guaranteed to be a success. Although Jimmy was enjoying his freedom to contribute his talent to many charitable causes, he should have been taking it easy. Eventually, nature called him to a halt again, and in March 1975 jaundice was diagnosed. He slowly recovered from this and was soon out and about visiting friends and relatives. One of the people he visited in Dundee's Ninewells Hospital in August was Mrs Isobel Binnie, 'wee Isa' from the Dundee Denham family. Jimmy was one of her first visitors and, when he was leaving, he asked the ward sister if he could bring his box on his next visit. The sister readily agreed and, when he next appeared, he played for an hour in Ward 16, while patients from other wards were wheeled in to listen. A quote from the time describes the scene:

> As reel tumbled out on the heels of strathspey, the domestic staff began to dance at the end of the ward. A husband who called to visit his wife couldn't believe his eyes. Her progress back to health had been slow. Now she was sitting up doing a sort of Highland hand-jive. One woman went over and shook Jimmy's hand. 'I've wanted to do this for years,' she said. He spent more than ten minutes signing get-well cards. Jimmy has now retired from showbusiness, but the magic of his 'dunt' persists.

A few days later Jimmy was in Bridge of Earn Hospital to have his gall bladder removed.

He made sure that he took his box with him and when asked if he used it he said, 'Oh aye – we had a bit o a sing sang the nicht afore my operation. Then, later, in bed this new tune came tae me. It was complete afore I fell asleep; a pipe march. I gave it a name right away: *Jimmy Shand's Compliments to Mr A.J.M. Mathieson* – the surgeon wha was tae operate on me next day.' The operation was successful but Jimmy was banned from playing his big accordion for quite a while afterwards.

Once he had recovered, another LP was recorded in Edinburgh, and Jimmy found that the old magic was still there, ready to be released through his fingertips. In 1976, Jimmy's friend, author David Phillips, produced a book based on Jimmy's life. This was printed by D. Winter and Son of Dundee, but for some inexplicable reason only 700 copies were completed – the book therefore had a very limited distribution. Erskine had better news as far as the prospects of his playing was concerned. An operation on his hand had proved to be successful and he was practising again. As the news got round that he might be back, the bookings began to build up and he decided to give up his shop. Because of his health and the fact that Anne had not been very well, Jimmy, Anne and David moved into a bungalow, which he had helped to build, in front of Braidleys.

The *retired* Jimmy flew to the United States for a special charity performance, at the request of an old friend, and in 1977 was persuaded to do a limited tour of Australia, with The Alexander Brothers and other Scottish artistes. The following year Jimmy was kept busy, mainly with charitable events and hospital visits, which did not receive massive publicity but gave him a great deal of satisfaction. He was informed he was to receive a special gold disc, and went to Edinburgh on 29 November for the presentation. The award had just been handed to him by Ramon Lopez, the Managing Director of EMI Records, when a tall Irishman interrupted the ceremony and said, 'Thank you Ramon Lopez. Jimmy you weren't expecting a second presentation, but I came along here so that I could say, musician, conductor, award-winning musician, tonight Jimmy Shand – This Is Your Life!' The Irishman, of course, was

This is Your Life
(l–r): Ramon Lopez, Jimmy Shand and Eamonn Andrews

Eamonn Andrews and when the surprised Jimmy finally found his voice he said, 'Very nice, thank you.' It was a pleasant evening and Jimmy was seen by millions of television viewers laughing and smiling. Actor and comedian Jimmy Logan referred to the tour that he and Jimmy had made to Canada and the United States, and how after each show there was always a large crowd outside Jimmy's dressing room. 'They all seemed to be relatives or friends, he must have had a very good bike,' said Jimmy Logan. He continued: 'When I was in Australia, I went back stage after Jimmy's show but could not get near his dressing room. Later I was watching a parade which lasted for hours and involved thousands of people. A friend of mine said to me, 'I wonder where they have all come from?' and my reply was 'Jimmy Shand's dressing room.' Andy Stewart paid tribute to Jimmy and said, 'We not only love Jimmy, we are very proud of him because he has kept alive a tradition of Scottish music, a tradition of the makars and of Robert Burns, and a tradition that means a great deal to a great many of us. And we are delighted to see, in this day and age, the resurgence of the fiddle and accordion clubs throughout Scotland, a fantastic thing this to all of us who love our own music and I know to Jimmy as well. If it wasna for Jimmy, you wouldn't get these brilliant young lads coming along and playing the music they do. Jimmy, from all of us, for your music, thank you very much indeed.' The programme finished with Ian Powrie, who had come all the way from Australia, and some former members of Jimmy's band, playing a tune. The final touch was when Jimmy's grand-daughter Diane danced a jig to the music.

1979 was an eventful year for the 71 year-old Fifer and included another trip to Australia. Two new long playing records were produced and issued with the contrasting titles 'The Golden Years of Jimmy Shand' and 'The New Sound of Jimmy Shand'. A special evening for Jimmy was when he was the guest of honour at the National Association of Accordion & Fiddle Clubs' Annual Dinner. Over 200 musicians and friends gathered in Perth to honour the man who had become a legend in his lifetime.

The main speaker was Andy Stewart who immediately let loose with a broadside of jokes, stories and anecdotes. He apologised for being late and said that even if two of his other cars or, as he put it, his other two cars, had broken down, his wife Sheila and himself would have walked from Stonehaven just to be in such elite company. He said it was a great honour to have been asked to be the main speaker on such a special night and that the night would long be remembered in the annals of the history of Scotland's music, when those of Jimmy's own fraternity set aside a few hours to welcome this unique individual. Andy then asked everyone to be upstanding and to drink a toast to Jimmy Shand.

The chairman, Jimmy Blue, rose and, with some emotion in his voice, addressed Jimmy saying, 'From the National Association of Accordion and Fiddle Clubs please accept this as a wee something that you have done for all of us.' At that, the lights were dimmed, the spotlight came on, the curtain was pulled and there were gasps of delight when a full portrait in oils was revealed. This was Jimmy, in his Highland regalia, and on the table beside him was his Shand Morino – a truly magnificent picture. The applause was long and sincere and when it eventually died down Jimmy rose to speak. He was clearly overcome. His first words were: 'I don't understand how I deserved this.' Such is the man's humility.

He felt that when he retired he would have nothing to do. 'God knows how I find time to do nothing.' He then said that he had personally bought every box he ever had, and felt that if someone or some firm had gifted one he wouldn't be truly happy with it. 'When I accepted the invitation I never thought that it would be such a lavish affair. I thought just a quiet ceremony, with a few friends. However, if it gives you satisfaction then I accept in the same spirit. Thank you one and all and prosperity to all clubs in the future.' He was given a standing ovation.

Andy Stewart, although he had made his main speech, felt constrained to reply and his opening sentence was typical

Andy Stewart. 'It's a beautiful portrait and a great likeness Jimmy, you're almost smiling.' He went on to say that Jimmy had, in his own way, made a beautiful speech and was taken by the thought that Jimmy stood for his nation; and it was also a wonderful confession when Jimmy had said he had paid for every box he ever owned. He said, 'I don't think you can achieve the success Jimmy has without first having the gift, given by a higher power, and by paying for everything as you go along.' He went on: 'What a tremendous night this has been, it's warm in here, not just the heat of the room, but of the warmth of love and affection we have for one another and what we stand for – and that is the music of Scotland and that is Jimmy Shand.' Among the others who contributed to the evening were Jack Cooper, Angus Fitchet, Bobby MacLeod, Sandy Tulloch, Jim MacLeod, Bobby Colgan and Robert Whitehead. The rest of the evening was taken up by a ceilidh starring Angus Fitchet, John Clark, The Currie Brothers, Jimmy Yeaman, Bill Black and others. Even Jimmy played the box, much to everyone's delight.

In 1980, another LP was produced called 'A Tribute to Jimmy Shand – The First 46 Years'; and in the following year he produced one more LP called 'Scotland My Home'. All of this

The 'Muchty Trio – Diane Shand, Bruce Lindsay and David Shand

time he continued his routine of playing for folk in hospitals and for charities. In 1982 a rather special LP was issued; special in the sense that it not only contained Jimmy and his band, together with tenor James Urquhart, but it also included two unusual performers: one was Robbie Shepherd, who had by this time established a very successful broadcasting career based on the promotion of

Scottish Country Dance Music, and the other was Diane Shand, Jimmy's grand-daughter. Robbie sang some bothy ballads in his fine Aberdeen voice, while Diane gave a rendering of *The Lord of the Dance* which had been arranged by Jimmy. Diane was to appear in another LP the following year in recognition of Jimmy's 50th recording year. The other guests in this production were Ian Powrie and Bill Torrance. Diane did not appear alone, however; she was part of what was called 'The 'Muchty Trio' – she played the accordion, as did Bruce Lindsay, and the drums were played by her Uncle David, Jimmy's son. Jimmy's 50 years of accordion playing was also commemorated by the presentation of a special gold disc from Craighall Studio Productions.

The time was passing so quickly and the 'retired' Jimmy was so busy that another year passed before anyone had noticed, but in 1985 there were several things which came to public prominence. On 10 May at a ceremony held at Oban Station, a diesel electric locomotive was named 'Jimmy Shand'. The idea for this initiative came from Willie Laird, who had first met Jimmy Shand on the platform at Cupar railway station when he was fifteen. Jimmy had been travelling to London for a recording session with his band, while Willie was starting on the road (or rather rails) to achieving his ambition to become an engine driver. As the years went on, Willie had recurring thoughts that he would like to see Jimmy's name on a railway locomotive, and was delighted when eventually Chris Green, the General Manager of ScotRail, agreed to adopt his proposal.

Jimmy, his family and friends decided to make a long weekend out of their visit to Oban and he was involved in several other public engagements during that time. One was to present prizes in a local school's art competition, in which the school children had taken the railway as their theme. Another was to meet and give words of encouragement to groups of handicapped children. In the evenings he played publicly again, accompanied by many prominent Scottish country dance musicians, including Bobby McLeod. Mrs Shand-Kydd, who

The 'Jimmy Shand', Oban Station, June 1985

lived locally, presented prizes to the winners in the dancing competitions. On the way back home from this rather hectic few days, Jimmy indulged his love of the sea by paddling in the water and collecting chucky stanes.

In July, at the University of Dundee, Jimmy was presented with an Honorary Master of Arts degree. In his Laureation Address, promoting Jimmy for the honour, Professor J.B. Caird summarised Jimmy's life before going on to say:

> Scottish dance music would never have reached the high standard or popularity it now has, nor would Scottish country dancing have gained the interest of ordinary people, but for Jimmy Shand. With his button-key accordion he has combined the two traditions of Scottish country dance and music, and in doing so has made the same major contribution as Niel Gow and Scott Skinner before him. Although one of the greatest individual soloists of his generation, this kind and self-effacing man has mainly confined his solo playing to entertaining patients in hospitals and old people's clubs – his greatest pleasure is doing something for others.

Now we in this University wish to honour this great Master of Scottish dance music, who has always given enormous pleasure to Scots and adopted Scots, at home and abroad, and I would now invite you, My Lord and Chancellor, to confer on Jimmy Shand the degree of Master of Arts.

The Chancellor, The Rt. Hon. The Earl of Dalhousie, very happily performed the ceremony.

Jimmy Shand is presented with an Honorary Master of Arts degree by The Rt. Hon. The Earl of Dalhousie (the Chancellor at that time)
(© Dundee University)

Jimmy was keeping himself very fit by pottering around his house, and even digging a well to ensure a better water supply for Erskine's house. There were, of course, all his regular visits to friends, and to folk he did not know in hospital and nursing homes who were soon to become friends. In January 1986, Jimmy and Anne celebrated their Golden Wedding anniversary surrounded by family and friends. The event was held in Letham Village Hall and there were none of the last minute problems experienced at the Silver Wedding. One special item produced on the night was a cake made in the shape and colours of a Shand Morino accordion.

Jimmy and Anne's Golden Wedding

It was now almost expected by the buying public to be able to purchase a new Jimmy Shand LP every year, and in 1986 two were produced. More records followed in 1987, and in 1988 there were several radio and television broadcasts and interviews on the occasion of Jimmy's eightieth birthday, which renewed interest among the general public in his career and in Scottish dance music.

In 1989 Jimmy was given another public honour, this time by North East Fife District Council. Their illuminated heraldic presentation scroll read as follows:

> At Cupar on the Second day of June, Nineteen hundred and eighty nine. Which day the NORTH EAST FIFE DISTRICT COUNCIL, in pursuance of a Resolution passed at a meeting of the Council held on the twentieth day of December Nineteen hundred and eighty eight, did and do hereby admit and receive Jimmy Shand Esquire – Member of the Order of the British Empire – to be an HONORARY FREEMAN OF THE DISTRICT OF NORTH EAST FIFE with all rights, privileges and immunities thereto belonging in recognition of his giving great entertainment and enjoyment to the people of North East Fife and throughout the world and whose fame has done much to engender feelings of local pride.

For a man who had confessed to never really having a birthday party before his 70th, Jimmy now found that 28 January each year was used as a great excuse for all his friends and neighbours to have a get-together, and maybe a couple of tunes. He had also got into the habit of attending various Scottish Country Dance Music and Accordion Society AGMs, and in some of these he was occasionally persuaded to strap on a box again; and when he did there seemed to be an extra spring in the dancers' feet. It was also becoming more and more a case of the Shands' playing host to a seemingly increasing number of people, as folk from not only Britain but abroad, 'just happened to be passing and thought they would pop in.'

Perth AGM, June 1991

Back row (l–r): Jack Cooper, Anne & Jimmy Shand, Andy Stewart, Leila Powrie, Jimmy Blue, Joan Blue, Ian Powrie, Esme Shepherd; Front row (l–r): Robbie Shepherd, Jim Johnston, Bobby Colgan

A rare photo of Jimmy laughing at drummer and comedian, Bobby Colgan

Jimmy was asked in June 1990 by Jimmy Jr. to join him and a few musicians in making a music video. The recording itself seemed to go well and everybody looked forward to seeing the finished product.

In July 1992 Jimmy was invited to a special event held in Rossie Priory, then the home of Robert Spencer, cousin of Diana, Princess of Wales, and Earl Spencer. The occasion was the presentation of an Honorary Fellowship of the British College of Accordionists. The scroll said the Honorary Fellowship had been conferred upon Jimmy Shand MBE, MA:

> In genuine appreciation of all he has done for the good name of the accordion by the lifelong application of his masterly talents – for the enjoyment of all. It is the unanimous desire of the governing council that he be assured of the greatest esteem in which he is held by the college, as well as by lovers of the instrument the world over.

Jimmy was deeply touched by this honour, as it was another recognition by his peers of his work. It is appropriate that the long playing record issued in 1992 should be called *The One and Only Jimmy Shand.* One of the principal organisers of the Honorary Fellowship Award was Francis Wright, a friend of Jimmy's for over fifty years. Jimmy and Francis had collaborated in many musical publishing projects during this time and Francis was always a very welcome visitor to the Shand home.

Jimmy continued to be available to the organisers of many charities and was happy to contribute his services to many worthwhile causes. There was the occasional public performance, but not in any professional capacity. More honours were showered upon him from various organisations and enthusiastic friends.

On 15 January 1995 a special 'Shand Morino Day' was

organised at the Windygates Institute, in Fife, by Dave Black and Bruce Lindsay, great friends and enthusiasts of Jimmy's music. There were 59 Morino accordions on show and played on the day, including the very first four Shand Morino accordions, as well as an example of the last type produced in 1975. The organisers wanted to show their appreciation for Jimmy and his music, and for what he had done to encourage so many people over so many years. They said they were overwhelmed by the number of people that had turned up, and it was a great gathering for some folk to renew old acquaintances. The sound in the hall when all the musicians got into their stride was quite unique, and it was a great pity that the day had not been broadcast, although Valda Hood-Chin and her husband Alistair Hood did manage to record some interviews on tape. Jimmy, Anne and David moved through the crowds in a most unassuming way, and thoroughly enjoyed the event.

Windygates Shand Morino Day with four original Shand Morinos on display
Back row (l–r): Jim Edwards, Jimmy Shand;
Front row (l–r): David Simpson, Sandy Tulloch, Angus Oliver
(© Ron Stephen)

Due to unforeseen circumstances there had been a delay in the production of the music video which had been recorded in 1990, but it finally appeared in October 1995.

In 1995 a decision was made to commission a portrait of Jimmy Shand, and the citizens of Fife were invited to subscribe to its cost. George Bruce, President of the Royal Society of Portrait Painters, was chosen to undertake the commission. This caused a little stushie among Fife Regional Councillors, as they felt there should have been greater consultation before appointing the artist, but the Council still contributed. Lord Elgin, who organised the project, said, 'We simply didn't have time to play around with niceties and drawing up shortleets and the like.' As Jimmy said himself, 'You better get me on a canvas or I might be on a slab.' During the painting of the portrait Jimmy was not very well, but rallied for each sitting and was fit enough to be available, with the support of his family, at the official presentation in January 1996, on the shores of the Forth at East Wemyss. He declined to keep the painting in his own house, as he was concerned about security, but agreed that it should be hung in the National Portrait Gallery in Edinburgh, alongside that of Niel Gow.

Jimmy and Anne celebrated their Diamond Wedding anniversary in January 1996 at the Burnside Hotel, Newburgh, and again it was a night enjoyed by relatives and friends, some of whom had travelled quite a distance to be there. On 16 October, the British Academy of Songwriters, Composers and Authors awarded Jimmy the Academy's Gold Badge of Merit. This was in recognition of Jimmy's often unheralded skill at composing tunes and his prodigious output.

The Shand house in Auchtermuchty continues to be a magnet for Scottish dance music enthusiasts from all over the world, and in the following chapter there are many comments from people who have 'taken the road to Fife'. As an example, on Sunday 28 September 1997, two days before this book was due to be handed to the publishers, Donald Ring and his wife, having the unusual luxury of a free weekend, came across from Ireland and popped in to see Jimmy, Anne and David. As I left they were preparing to go out for a meal and talk over old times, and no doubt old tunes.

The Shand family in 1980

Twelve

During the research for this book I have come across many tributes to Jimmy Shand, some by people who have since died. I have included examples of what they said, as they reflected the great reservoir of enthusiasm for Jimmy as a man and for his contribution to music. I have also been very fortunate in being able to speak to and visit many others who, without exception, expressed their willingness to be quoted and involved with this publication.

The special quality of Jimmy's playing was recognised by many people when he was still quite young but one person, Jock Turpie, a local comedian and raconteur, must have had a prophetic vision when he wrote this obviously sincerely-felt tribute:

The Wemyss has aye been famous for its castles an its lairds,
Its ruins an past histories o kail an ither yairds;
But still mair famous it's become, admired through a' the
    land,
For on the Wemyss was born an bred a chap called
    Jimmy Shand.

I met him at the puir hoose, aye, twenty years ago,
A striplin, he was awfu blate, an sweer tae mak his bow;
But on the stage he tampit, man the fingerin was grand,
I could see the hall-mark stampit on that laddie
    Jimmy Shand.

He's playin tae the puir fowk yet, a million fans he's got,
Whaurever there's a wireless set, whaurever there's a Scot;
The pensioner – his crookit stick becomes a magic wand
As he chaps the flair an whistles, keepin time tae
    Jimmy Shand.

He has scores o imitators, but they dinna hae the lilt –
They mind ye o a piper on the march withoot his kilt;
But tae him it's a' sae simple, an it trickles up yer gland
When ye hear auld Kate Dalrymple introducin
    Jimmy Shand.

So let's forget oor troubles nae maitter hoo we feel;
Pit on a record, lassie, an we'll hae the eightsome reel;
Life's no the problem it wid seem if we could just
    understand,
So tak yer pairtners an God Bless the Wemyss for gien us
    Jimmy Shand.

GEORGE CHISHOLM, the internationally famous trombone player commented: 'When someone asks: "Which are your three favourite bands", I say Count Basie, Duke Ellington and Jimmy Shand and they can't understand this, and say, "What do you mean," to which I reply, "Listen to Jimmy Shand and you'll find your feet – the tremendous beat – it's the teedle dum deedle dum – you will find your feet going and there's a swing to it".'

JOHN CARMICHAEL, the well-known Scottish musician, accompanied Jimmy on a tour of Australia in the 1970s. Because of union regulations there had to be a certain proportion of Australian musicians in the company. John was put in charge of the band and introduced the performers. On one occasion at the Sydney Opera House he introduced 'The Legendary Jimmy Shand' and the whole audience rose to their feet and clapped and cheered. Jimmy came on and stood at the microphone for over five minutes before turning to John and saying 'I wish they would stop that son 'til we get a wee tune going.'

Another story from John, confirmed by Ian Powrie, concerns the accommodation arrangements. Ian Powrie admits to occasionally liking a wee dram, but knowing Jimmy did not drink he did not want him to feel uncomfortable when they were sharing a room. The solution was to pour some whisky into a Listerine bottle, which he could have to hand at night.

One night in the hotel there was a shortage of glasses and Ian asked if he could use Jimmy's. 'Aye son, jist tak ma teeth oot the glass and use it,' Jimmy replied. Jimmy was not fooled with what had been going on and said, with a twinkle in his eye, 'Yer havin a lot o trouble wi yer throat, son!'

Jimmy, Ian Powrie, the Alexander Brothers and John Carmichael were among the guests at an open-air barbecue, when they were asked what they would like to eat. Tom Alexander wanted steak diane and his brother Jack asked for peppered steak. Jimmy's reply was, 'Have ye got ony mince – I wid luv tae hae a steak, but I canna chow it wi ma teeth.'

In New Zealand in the 1970s they still had the old fashioned phone system whereby international calls were booked through an operator. As they had been touring for a while, Jimmy decided to phone home and asked John Carmichael if he would get the number. After a considerable while, including having to spell Auchtermuchty several times, John got through and Jimmy stepped in to the phone box to speak. He was there for a while and when he came out, Ross Bowie, the Alexander Brothers' agent, jokingly asked Jimmy if he had been phoning New York to set up another tour. Jimmy had obviously got his priorities right when he replied, 'Na – ye ken it's rainin in 'Muchty?'

Actor and comedian JIMMY LOGAN remembers a tour with Jimmy in Canada. They had finished the show and looked forward to a few days rest. The town they were staying in had a church with a big stone altar, and was used by three denominations. Living above the church was a family, which included two daughters who each had an accordion, and Jimmy spent his two days' 'holiday' repairing and tuning the instruments, improvising tools from anything to hand.

During this tour, the Scots were invited to be part of an audience at a performance by a Scottish country dance group. When the performance was finished, the touring party was asked to entertain and without any fuss Jimmy got up and soon had the place hooching. Jimmy Logan recalls being at the ceremony when Jimmy was given the Freedom of North East Fife at Cupar. After his short speech, Jimmy Shand joined former band members for a few tunes. Jimmy Logan described that, when he watched this white-haired group and listened to their unique rendering of *Bonnie Dundee,* he could see tears of emotion welling in many eyes.

Jimmy Logan was at a Highland Games in Rothesay and turning to his friend Johnny Beattie, remarked how lucky entertainers were in that they touched people, and how it is certainly true of Jimmy Shand who has touched so many people throughout the world.

IAN POWRIE, who has known Jimmy since the early 1930s, remembers that, when Jimmy was working with Forbes, he used to pop in to see his father if he was in the area. Ian's dad was a grieve, and the family lived in a tied cottage; money was not exactly growing on trees. Jimmy always seemed to time his visits to be near tea time and would say he had a taste for fish and chips. Without any fuss, he would go down to Laird's Fish and Chip shop in Blairgowrie and bring back enough for everyone in the family. Sometimes Jimmy would arrive driving a Norton motorbike and would say to the young impressionable Ian, 'Like a wee run on the back o the bike son?' Ian comments, 'It used to take me days to recover, he's an awfa man for the speed ye know.'

At the presentation of his portrait at East Wemyss, Jimmy was sitting quietly playing some tunes and Ian commented on how well the box sounded to which Jimmy replied, 'I'm no likely to get ony better noo.'

When referring to Jimmy, Ian Powrie admits, 'He has terrific powers of concentration. The extra grace notes create magic. There is naebody, nor will there ever be anybody, who could take his place.'

At a concert in Australia, Ian asked Jimmy back on to the stage to play a few tunes. As Jimmy walked to the microphone, Ian encouraged the audience to loosen their stays and get up and dance in the aisles. This they did with great enthusiasm, singing along to the music. After the playing was over Jimmy spoke to Ian and said 'Ye'll no need tae be doin that again, son, in a concert, it spiles the music!'

IAN HOLMES, the Scottish country dance musician from Dumfries, recalls, 'I first met Jimmy around 1953 when he and his fiddler Syd Chalmers were walking down English Street in Dumfries. I was introduced to him by my girlfriend Margaret Bell, who was later to become my wife. After that, when we went to his dances, Jimmy would sometimes invite me to sit in with the band. Later in 1962, when doing my first broadcast with my own band for the BBC, Jimmy came into the Edinburgh studio to wish us good luck. Imagine one of the biggest names in show business, well known throughout the world, yet taking the time to offer us a few words of encouragement.

'Stan Saunders who was on double bass was actually a member of Jimmy's band, but Jimmy always insisted that Stan should do our broadcasts even though it meant he had the problem of getting someone to deputise. On occasions this was not possible and the Shand Band played minus a bass player.

'I never forgot his kindness which, of course, was so typical of the man, but it was not until 1995 that I had the pleasure of arranging and playing a programme in which all the tunes were composed by Jimmy. For this very special broadcast we were joined on fiddle by Ian Powrie, himself a long time friend of Jimmy's.'

IAN COLLIE, the former Director of Education for Central Region recalls, 'On a Sunday evening, when I was a boy in the late 1940s, several of us used to gather in a farm bothy to listen to Jimmy Shand records and then we would set to on our melodeons. He was a folk hero then, as now, and so it was a great thrill eventually to meet him when I was Director of Education for Central Region. Jimmy had come, in 1980, to visit our Day of Scottish Dance for school pupils, accompanied by Robert Innes of Stirling University, who founded the Heritage of Scotland Summer Schools (to promote Scottish culture). A particular memory is of an occasion soon after that, when Robert organised a trip to Tobermory to make a video recording of Bobby McLeod, and he took Jimmy and me with him. We were cautiously negotiating roadworks near Dalmally on the way down when a great yellow bulldozer suddenly started reversing in our direction, and Robert had to reverse also, in great haste. Jimmy, in the front seat, had a particularly good view of this huge thing looming over us, and his customary reticence was abandoned in favour of a very earthy utterance indeed! Many a time afterwards he laughed about that day. For too long, Scottish music and dance were neglected by the education system, and a great debt is owed to Jimmy Shand for sustaining popular interest so that today a much more positive and better informed attitude prevails.'

VALDA HOOD-CHIN, research broadcaster and founder of SCOTSPEAK relates, 'As far back as I can remember I have always been a lover of radio. I can picture myself as a youngster, almost 50 years ago, sitting in the front room of our house in Wimbledon on a Saturday night with my ear pressed firmly against the speaker of our old Bakelite wireless set so as to catch the final, precious moments of Jimmy Shand and his Scottish Dance Band broadcast "live" on the BBC Light Programme every weekend – twiddling the volume knob right up to a maximum, in a vain attempt to preserve the last remaining, distorted, seconds of a fading accumulator battery before the familiar, much loved strains of Jimmy's music melted away into the ether.

'Suffice to say at the tender age of five I knew next to nothing about music and, what's more, was completely ignorant about the cultural aspect of Scottish music and even to the whereabouts of Scotland! However, what I did know was that I was listening to something unique and exciting, and from then on became a fan and regular listener to Jimmy's programmes.

'Imagine therefore my delight, some years later, as a fully-fledged BBC broadcaster, being introduced to the great man himself whilst recording in Fife at 'The Morino Day' – an event, held at Windygates Community Hall in celebration of (and as a tribute to) Jimmy Shand. Arranged by his fellow Fifers, musicians and devotees who, for a lifetime, have been enthused by Jimmy's musicianship and playing techniques, they stated, "He's a legend in his own lifetime... so why not show our appreciation now whilst he is still with us and can enjoy his music with us?"

'I must admit that I've been surprised at how little has been written about Jimmy, who is known and admired throughout the world for his own distinctive brand of Scottish music, which bridges all race and cultural differences, and unites us in a mutual love for a "good tune", transporting us back to the days of innocent enjoyment.'

BILLY ANDERSON, the accomplished musician and broadcaster, remembers, 'My earliest memory of Jimmy Shand goes back to the 1950s when, as a very young accordionist, I visited the great man at the family home in Auchtermuchty. I remember travelling by car with my adopted Mum and Dad, Isabella and John Tulloch of Priorletham, who brought me up and encouraged me to take an interest in music and who, from their earlier years in the farming and mining areas of Fife, knew Mr and Mrs Jimmy Shand on a personal basis.

'In 1964 I was invited to play "second box" with Jimmy Shand Junior and his band, travelling to venues all over Scotland in a rather plush Bedford Dormobile, appearing and performing with various noted musicians such as Jimmy Ritchie, Syd Chalmers, Jack Delaney, Jimmy Scott, Stan Saunders and Billy Thom. One particular gig which I distinctly remember, was appearing on stage at the Kelvin Hall in Glasgow on Saturday 11 April 1964, at the Scottish Food Exhibition, where I can still see the large red letters on the entertainment banner which read, "The Jimmy Shand Show featuring Jimmy Shand Junior and his band".

'One of the finest musical compliments I ever received

happened on a recent visit to the Shand household, when Jimmy informed me that he had just published a new collection of his latest compositions, the music publication of which he very kindly presented to me. Being a reader of music, I immediately opened the shiny booklet and proceeded to sight read the melodies penned by the man himself. He promptly announced that he would just get the box and let me hear them. On his return from the adjacent room, he sat down in his chair, placed the small button accordion on his knee and without securing the shoulder straps, proceeded to play the tunes as written in the book, which I still held in my hand. Unable to resist the musical opportunity, I opened a nearby accordion case, containing a small piano accordion, which I began to play in unison with Jimmy as he played.

'There we were, the two of us. Jimmy Shand, well into his eighties, with a small button box, playing his own compositions, straight from his remarkable musical memory; and there was I, sitting opposite, with a borrowed piano accordion, playing his tunes, as written in the printed music sheet in front of me, note for note, as if it was rehearsed. I'll never forget that feeling of musical satisfaction, when, as we played the final chord together, he looked up and said, "My God, laddie, ye can fairly read the music!"

'Over the years, Scottish music has taken me all over the world – United States of America, Canada, United Arab Emirates, Oman, Brunei, Sarawak, Australia, various parts of the continent – and also provided the opportunity over the past fifteen years to present Scottish music on a regular basis with Radio Tay in Dundee, where my incoming mail continues to contain requests for the "legendary" Jimmy Shand.'

ROBBIE SHEPHERD who, over the years, has had many dealings with Jimmy, remembers his first professional contact in the Tivoli Theatre in Aberdeen. Robbie was MC for the evening and was very nervous, so he asked Jimmy how he should introduce him, by name or by tune. Jimmy said, 'It had better be by name, laddie, as the tune is, *Dr Ross's Fiftieth Welcome to the Argyll Gathering.'*

Robbie also testified to the fact that Jimmy always liked a hearty breakfast with jars of honey and marmalade on the table, and a large container with butter. There was one particular eating establishment, which Jimmy regularly frequented, which had gone all modern, and supplied the preserves and butter in small plastic containers. Jimmy picked up the honey container, called the waitress across and said, 'I see ye keep a bee!'

JOHN DREEVER mentions how he first became aware of Jimmy. 'Jimmy Shand's music first came to Westray via "78" records on the wind-up gramophone and the radio. I can remember listening to the "Two Greats", Jimmy Shand and Harry Lauder on New Year's night. He came to Westray as part of a tour of Orkney, shortly after the war, and played at a dance in St George's Hall. On hearing him play on that occasion, I decided that I wanted to play the button-box rather than the piano accordion.

'I next met Jimmy Shand in the mid-fifties when he did a tour of Orkney with his band, accompanied by Anne and Laura Brand. Since the sixties I've been involved in dance music and Jimmy Shand's tunes have formed a considerable part of our repertoire and have been very popular for the local dances.

'My daughter went to Auchtermuchty for the Folk Festival in the 1980s and she and a friend were looking for the local bank. As she walked out of a newsagent's, she was surprised to see her friend talking to Jimmy Shand and was astonished to discover that he didn't know who was giving him directions. She couldn't recall a time in her life when she *hadn't* known that there was a Jimmy Shand!

'In 1993 I met Jimmy Shand in his home and was privileged to hear him playing by his fireside. To hear him in his own home was a pleasure never to be forgotten.'

JIM QUIGLEY first met Jimmy at a dance in Mid Calder in the 1950s. The hall was so packed that the organisers had to turn folk away, but Jim managed to get Jimmy to play his request item *De'il Amang the Tailors*. Jim remembers attending the Ideal Home Exhibition in the old Waverley Market, Edinburgh, just to stand and listen to the regular performances of Jimmy Shand and his Band. The more he listened, the more he came to realise that Jimmy had something which he had *always* had, something given to just a few – a special genius. Jim was reminded of a quotation attributed to Scott Skinner: 'Talent does what it can, genius does what it must'.

In 1992 the annual dinner of the National Farmers' Union was being held in the Dunblane Hydro. Jim Quigley was one of those in the Fife and Kinross branch who were responsible for organising the event. A few months before, Jim had spoken to Erskine about the possibility of his father playing. Erskine's advice was not to say anything, as his father might worry about it, but to mention it much nearer the time. This Jim did and when asked, Jimmy thought about it for a few minutes and then asked, 'Is it for you Jim?' When Jim nodded, Jimmy said, 'Och aye, I'll dae it.' Nobody knew that Jimmy was going to appear, and on the night of the dinner on 7 March, after the meal and the speeches, the announcement was made, 'Ladies and Gentlemen, we are proud to announce a special appearance of the legendary Jimmy Shand.' The curtains were pulled back to reveal Jimmy sitting with the band, and the hall erupted in applause. Jim also remembers how Jimmy fairly gave advice and encouragement. On one occasion when Jim was attempting a tune on a box in Jimmy's house, an impromptu lesson was given. Jimmy had nodded approval as to what Jim was doing and then said, 'Jist a wee thing here an there like – jist keep the box on,' and got up and stood behind Jim, stretched his arms through between his, grasped the box and said, 'Yer no cross bassin and yer no phrasin.'

JIMMY BLUE recalls his first professional meeting with Jimmy Shand in the Aytoun Hall, Auchterarder, in 1950. The occasion was a dance, the music was fine, the folk were hooching, but Jimmy was preoccupied as he sidled across to Jimmy Blue and said with great solemnity, 'A dinna ken whit I'm gonna dae, I've forgot ma keys.' Jimmy Blue's wife, Joan, remembers in particular the presentation of the painting at East Wemyss, as well as each of the occasions when Jimmy Shand and she shared a professional platform. 'No matter where we were, sometime in the evening he would turn to me when I was playing the piano and give me a lovely smile.'

BOBBY CROW, the well known Scottish band leader, remembers he first met Jimmy when he was nineteen years old. Bobby had started 'The Olympians' and was appearing in the RAF Hall at Leuchars in Fife. The hall was a long narrow place and someone said it was a pity it did not have more speakers. Jimmy asked Andy Gow, the band's bus driver, to go out to the bus and bring in some extra speakers to enable the dancers to hear the music in a more balanced way. Bobby said without any hesitation, 'If it had not been for Jimmy Shand there would have been no Scottish country dance music the way we know it today.'

BRYCE LAING, Jimmy's record producer since the mid-sixties, was given the responsibility of escorting Jimmy to the Caledonian Hotel in Edinburgh without making him aware that he was appear on 'This is Your Life'. Bryce remembers ushering Jimmy in through the side door, only to be approached by a well-known Scottish actor who said, 'Well, Jimmy, this is a wonderful night for you…' but before he could go any further Bryce gave him a sharp kick on the shins!

DONALD RING, the Irish musician, has got no doubts as to what he thinks about Jimmy Shand. When I asked him he described Jimmy as 'an absolute gentleman. He is the most under-rated genius on the accordion. Nobody will surpass what he has achieved with the instrument. He found his own way and was the standard bearer for those who came after him.'

Donald first saw Jimmy at the City Hall, Cork, in 1966 and was captivated by his music from the start. He also remembers writing to Jimmy enquiring about a box repair and addressed the package to 'Mr Jimmy Shand somewhere in Scotland' – and it arrived!

In 1979 Jimmy went across to Ireland to help Donald and his wife celebrate their 21st wedding anniversary. The event was held in Cork City Hall and the crowds were so large that the bronze glass doors were broken and Donald had to pay for the repair.

JIM RITCHIE has many memories of Jimmy, and refers to one story associated with Jimmy's music. W.C. Fields, the American film comedian, was appearing in Birmingham, and on his first night, in showbusiness terms, he was dying a death. The audience were becoming restless when Fields decided to play a Jimmy Shand record; thereafter, the audience erupted with clapping and cheering and he managed to leave the stage safely. For the rest of the week W.C. Fields ensured he had the record and gramophone available. Jim also remembers when Jimmy was appearing at an Irish club in Kilburn, London, the crowds were so large that riot police had to be called in and they admonished Jimmy for disturbing the peace. Jim still thinks this was unfair. One of Jim's earliest recollections of being aware of Jimmy Shand was through gramophone records, and remembers one occasion when he had been playing some records in a bothy for his friends when he misjudged their break time. The grieve, Bob Anderson, came along to find out what was keeping them, but he too stayed to listen to the records.

HARRY LAWSON can be very precise as to how long he has known Jimmy. It was 28 November 1934 when he went with some friends to Forbes' shop in Dundee to look at a little black dot accordion. Jimmy played a tune and then asked Harry if he played anything. When Harry said he played the fiddle, Jimmy suggested that he and his friends pop into Forbes' piano shop after tea. Harry used to go round the bothies on Jimmy's motorbike when he was selling accordions and remembers on one trip alone Jimmy sold four boxes. On another occasion, along the Arbroath Road, Jimmy was going so fast Harry asked him to stop, saying, 'I need tae go an change ma troosers.' In 1938 at the Angus Show in Brechin, Forbes had a stall displaying gramophones and melodeons. Next to the stall was a threshing mill, and Harry remembers when Jimmy played the box to the rhythm of the mill, the music brought tears to the eyes. Harry recalls that he often used to take Jimmy home to his mother's for a good country tea. Harry's father was a great whistler and on one occasion after whistling the *Rights o Man Reel*, Jimmy picked up the box and played the tune through. On the occasion of Harry and his wife's Golden Wedding in June 1990, Jimmy turned up for the celebration having written a tune which he called *The Dora Winifred Lawson March*.

PHIL CUNNINGHAM, the well known musician with a particular flair for the accordion, remembers, 'The number of times I must have listened to Jimmy Shand's records as a baby and as a toddler, must have had some kind of impression, some kind of subliminal suggestion; because I was given a toy accordion when I was about three, heading for four, and I actually played a tune on it when I got it, without anyone ever showing me how to do it. One of the first tunes I learned to play properly was the *Bluebell Polka*, which was one of the 78s my grandmother had. He has been a great influence, certainly in my earlier years. When I started to play professionally I had to develop a style different from Jimmy Shand, but retained a great respect for the man and his music. I remember on one occasion going to Auchtermuchty, sitting in the car for twenty minutes and then driving away without speaking to him. I held him in awe. Eventually I had the great privilege of playing the *Bluebell Polka* with Jimmy on the grass outside his house. There will never be another Jimmy Shand. I don't think anybody can lick his boots really, he has such an individual style of playing. Anybody trying to do it would be a poor copy.'

The *Bluebell Polka* was a significant milestone in the musical career of another musician of international repute. RICHARD MICHAEL, the widely respected music educationalist and musical director of the Fife Youth Jazz Orchestra remembers that it was the first tune he learned to play on the piano by ear. Richard said, 'Jimmy Shand is the best advert to persuade people to learn to read music.'

JIMMIE MACGREGOR the folk singer, broadcaster and long-distance walker recalls: 'I think, like a lot of other people, my earliest memories of the Shand sound were as a wee boy at school. In the gymnasium we were taught Scottish country dancing, which I hated at the time, but realised later it was quite a good thing – and we were dancing, or learning to dance, to the music of Jimmy Shand on records. It occurred to me later that this was happening all over the world; an awful lot of people, even generations of people, heard the music of Jimmy Shand and learned to dance to it.

'So far as the Scottish country dance music scene was concerned, with its dinner jackets and kilts, it seemed to some of us that it was rather formal – it was looked on as a bit couthie and stuffy; and I wouldn't say that the folk musicians of my era in the early days sneered at it, but they more or less ignored it, they rejected it, it was beneath their notice. I think they tended to forget that someone like Jimmy Shand, whose whole background was the traditional melodeon playing for self-made entertainment, was in a way the *genuine* traditional music, whereas the folkies were *trying* to be traditional. You cannot have another Jimmy Shand – he is a one-off.'

After one of his illnesses, when Jimmy had reconstructed a band, he insisted on doing an audition for the BBC. BEN LYONS, the famous BBC radio producer, remembers: 'I set up a studio in Glasgow, and Jimmy and the band came along and did an audition, and you know, this was my first really big job and I was petrified, because the band was not all it was cracked up to be; in fact it wasn't playing very well at all, and me being very, very new, and Jimmy having been in the business for so long, I didn't know quite how to cope with it. I didn't really have to bother too much because Jimmy insisted on coming into the listening room after he had done the audition. He heard the tapes, and was the first one to say, "Ah Ben, that's terrible, ye can't pass that", and that took the weight off my shoulders and I agreed with him. He asked if he could do another audition – the great Jimmy Shand asking me! He did another one, and the second time round it was absolutely first class, and the programme series, which was meant to be for thirteen weeks, went on from then for over 200 programmes on the Light Programme. They had repeats on the domestic service and they also went out on BBC World Service.

'The recording company EMI wanted to make a recording of these *Heather Mixture* programmes, but the BBC were not keen on their title being used, so another one was adopted called "Scottish Mixture". The recording featured, among others, Moira Anderson and Bill McCue, and has the quite unique sound of Jimmy Shand *singing*.

'Jimmy was very fond of cheese and often used the phrase "cheese for energy", and there was many a time after rehearsing in the BBC Edinburgh studios when the assembled company would pop round the corner to have a cheese dish called *chang wang* in the local restaurant. The thing about Jimmy Shand was his tempo was so consistent; if he recorded a piece of music in rehearsals at a certain time, it would be exactly the same time in the broadcast.'

SANDY MOIR played the piano in recordings Jimmy made in London in 1936. Sandy, who really was the pianist in band performances with Jim Cameron, joined Jimmy, Jim and Margaret Low in a recording session for Beltona. Margaret Low's aunt provided the accommodation, and a lot of improvisation was done so far as the music was concerned. It was quite an occasion to be in London, and as they were walking towards the studio, they tended to step off the pavement and had to be reminded they were no longer in Kirriemuir. In another trip to the studios, they used the train, and it wasn't until they were on their journey that it was brought to their attention that they were standing in a 'Ladies Only' compartment. Jimmy's response to this was to say, 'We'll jist say we thought it said lauddies.' Sandy has a very great affection for Jimmy, having first met him at the Kirriemuir Music Festival in 1934, and he remembers another occasion, many years later, when he was travelling in a car on tour with Robin Hall and Jimmie MacGregor. They were heading for Stornoway when they noticed a car sitting at the verge of the road and just as they passed it they all said at once 'That looks like Jimmy Shand!' They stopped and discovered that Jimmy had himself stopped to help another motorist. He was so concerned that the motorist would be all right, Jimmy waited until the AA arrived before completing his own journey.

The band leader JIM JOHNSTONE, who played with Jimmy many times, remembers other journeys. 'I had no idea until I arrived on the other side of the world just how big this man was in entertainment terms. The stadiums, the places we played in – we're talking about thousands of people coming along to hear Jimmy Shand and his band – and they were not all Scots people. He had, and still has, an appeal across the board.'

WILLIE MCKELVEY, who retired from being a Member of Parliament in May 1997, remembers many happy practice nights in his Mum and Dad's ground floor tenement in Dundee during the late 1940s and early 1950s. Willie is proud of the fact that his father, George, played the accordion with Jimmy for over 25 years, and even found it useful on one political occasion. At a Scottish Grand Committee meeting, Sir Nicholas Fairbairn appeared wearing tartan trews, while a fellow Tory MP, Bill Walker, wore a kilt. Willie rose to his feet and declared that, if he had realised that tartan was the uniform of the committee, he would have put on the kilt his father had worn when he played with Jimmy Shand.

THE PROCLAIMERS, the internationally famous pop duo, was

founded in Auchtermuchty by twins Craig and Charlie Reid. Charlie remembers being aware of Jimmy Shand when he and his family moved to the town in 1972. As he and his brother became interested in music, they got a great deal of help and encouragement every time they went into Erskine's shop, but they had their own particular ideas about musical style. Charlie used to hear a lot of Jimmy Shand recordings when he visited a friend's house, and sometimes wonders if he was subconsciously absorbing the timing, as some of the more recent Proclaimers' records have a dignified feel in waltz time. Charlie also added that in all their travelling, his brother and himself never heard a bad word about Jimmy, just respect.

One person with a great deal of respect for Jimmy is singer BILL McCUE, who has many fond memories of their times together. On a tour of Canada, Bill became Jimmy's hairdresser, and was responsible for booking all his telephone calls to Scotland. It was on this tour that Bill admits that Jimmy taught him a lesson without saying so. They used to share a car to and from the halls or theatres they were appearing in, and Bill sometimes had to wait for hours after a show while Jimmy spoke to all the people who wanted to see him. Bill has never forgotten what Jimmy said, when asked if he ever wished he could get away earlier, 'Son, these people are oor bread and butter!'

Bill also recalls one of the times he was asked to interview Jimmy on television. They had agreed between them not to talk about personalities, but the programme producers, knowing that Jimmy sometimes answered a question with one word, had some archive material ready to slot in if there was a lull in the conversation. On that particular evening, Jimmy was in fine form and Bill was surprised to hear the producer's voice in his earphone saying that they had 25 minutes in the can and they hadn't used any archive material. The producer then suggested Bill try an experiment and not say anything for 30 seconds. After 15 seconds Jimmy looked at Bill and, thinking 'Bill's forgotten what to say', continued, 'An offy nice fellow that Edmondo Ross.' This comment totally confused Bill and the production team, until Jimmy explained he had met the rumba band leader at the Carl Alan awards. So much for 'no personalities'!

BRENDAN BREEN, the Irish musician, is quite unstinting in his love and admiration for Jimmy, and declares he has been a fan for as long as he can remember. He talked about the time when he used to take home thirty shillings in his pay packet. Every week he had a set routine. A pound would go to his mother, and he would buy two records at three shillings and sixpence each, leaving three shillings to himself. If they were available, the records would be Jimmy Shand recordings. With a good Irish sense of awareness, Brendan recalls an occasion when Jimmy's music seemed out of this world. He was standing outside his house one clear night, watching a comet blazing in the sky. The windows were open and a Jimmy Shand record, the *Silver City Waltz,* was playing on the turntable. It occurred to Brendan that the tempo and the pitch of the recording seemed so appropriate to the visual spectacular. Only an Irishman could be so discerning.

JACK EMBLOW, the accordion wizard, was delighted to work as a session musician on some of Jimmy's London recordings. 'I arrived at the studio and Jimmy and the boys were there and they handed the music out. Of course I can sight read all right, and I played the part, but it was in no way the same as Jimmy played it. The Scottish stuff contains so many subtle accents and little embellishments, which I don't feel, and if you wrote them all out for me I could go home and practise them for two weeks and I still wouldn't sound like Jimmy Shand – everything he plays he swings.'

Another musician of international status is BERT WEEDON, the guitar genius, who also did some session work for Jimmy. He recalls, 'Jimmy gives the impression that his playing is all carefree and happy, which it is, but is also carefully thought out and performed. *Happy Days* was the name of the recording and they were happy days working with Jimmy Shand.'

BOB MCINTOSH, a friend of Jimmy's and a fair fiddle player in his own right, referred to some of Jimmy's interests which were not generally well known. Jimmy used to play at Probus functions, and contributed his time and his music to help Bob's work at Stratheden Hospital in Fife. The patients willingly did their exercises if Jimmy was there, and some would not go back to their rooms until he said goodbye. For three and a half years, after he retired, Jimmy went to exercise and self-defence classes on a Wednesday night, and only stopped when he broke his ankle one night while out walking his dog. Boxing and wrestling were also popular with Jimmy, and if they were on the television on a Saturday afternoon it was not worth visiting him. But more often than not visitors were always very welcome, and Bob remembers being in Jimmy's house when three lads from Canada knocked on the door, looking for an autograph. Jimmy welcomed them in and, when he discovered they were Cape Breton fiddlers on tour, he encouraged them to play and joined them on the box. They left an hour and a half later.

Another who can testify to the warmth of the welcome in the Shand house is JIM DOUGLAS. He remembers seeing Jimmy's Packard car outside a friend's house in Strathkinness, while a music lesson was underway inside, in the late 1940s. Eventually Jim's mother bought him his own box, and in 1966 he bought a Morino in Dundee, the day before the pound was devalued! Although he never played professionally, Jim liked going to the accordion clubs at Windygates and Letham, where he met Jimmy and started visiting him 'for a wee tune.' Jimmy Shand is, according to Jim, a 'famous son of Scotland and we are all proud of him.'

MALCOLM JONES, the lead guitarist with Runrig, comments, 'My earliest memory of Jimmy Shand was via a family LP. Teenage years saw the familiar rebellion against "tartan and haggis" music, with Jimmy Shand lumped in with that. My early on-stage appearances involved playing Scottish dance music, albeit with electric guitars and drum kit as the backdrop to the accordion. Gradually, I rediscovered the roots of the music, and realised Shand was not readily acknowledged outside the small dance band scene as the master musician he is. Shand's famous economy with words, and his refusal to intellectualise his music, has probably limited his appeal to the "enthusiasts", which is a shame, as in this day and age many "exotic" folk musicians are lauded for their innovation and patronised for being figureheads of their culture. Jimmy Shand has been ALL these. I was fortunate enough to witness his playing at close hand, and his legendary technique was a joy to behold, making the whole performance, as with all great musicians, seemingly effortless.'

A few years ago the international recording star RICHARD THOMPSON issued a record called *Don't sit on my Jimmy Shand's*. Many people thought that the recording was just making fun of Jimmy and his records, but if you read the lyrics, while they are very funny, they are in fact a homage to, and sincere appreciation of, Jimmy Shand's playing. Richard Thompson makes no secret of the fact he is most definitely a Jimmy Shand fan.

Jimmy Shand's support for charities, hospital visits and personal kindnesses are legendary, and too numerous to mention here but there was one occasion when the therapeutic value of his music was quite remarkable. Jimmy's own words are the best way to describe the situation. He recalls, 'She was a young nurse and she used to come to the dances. I played the Scots Guards' dances every year, always in January, for years and years. Going home from the dance one night, she was involved in a bad car accident and was so badly injured she fell into a coma. For weeks, lots o things were tried to bring her roon, and then her mither tried my records – she had been a lover o Shand music – and they seemed ta dae the trick. Imagine the surprise I got one night, when I was playing at the

Guards' dance, when this lassie walked across that hall, like a robot, but she walked herself, ye ken, kind o staggering – that was a great thing.'

This book is not big enough to record all the people Jimmy has met, has made music with, and received many kindnesses from over the years, but he wishes it to be made known they are always in his thoughts.

Much of what Jimmy has achieved would not have been possible without the love, support, and encouragement of his wife Anne, and his close and extended family. Having a solid foundation at home gave him the confidence to express his wonderful talent to millions of others.

Many people played with Jimmy over the years but, excluding those who occasionally sat in the band, following is a list of the musicians who regularly played in a Shand band:

Second Accordion
George McKelvey, Bert Shorthouse, Jim Johnstone, Jimmy Shand Jr.

Drums
Owen McCabe, Ian Wilson, Bobby Colgan, Len Kydd.

Fiddle
Dave Ireland, Angus Fitchet, Jim Ritchie, Syd Chalmers, George Muir.

Bass
Archie Oliphant, John White, Doug Maxwell, Dave Barclay, Gordon Lawson, Stan Saunders, John Strachan, Robin Brough.

Piano players and others
Peggy Edwards, Harry Forbes, Johnny Knight, Jimmy Scott, Ab Fields, Margaret Low, Norrie Whitelaw, Peter Straughan, David Barge, Jack Forsyth, Robin Brock, Archie Duncan, Davy Barrie.

Recordings

Charles S. Forbes recommended that Jimmy make a record in 1933. The recording company was Regal-Zonophone, and their studios were in Abbey Road in London. Three records were made but, because of technical faults, only two were issued:

The tunes included were:

Atholl Highlanders; Rakes of Kildare; Teviot Brig.	
Londonderry & High Level Hornpipes.	MR 1387
Punchbowl; My love she's but a lassie yet; The Fair Maid of Perth.	
Drunken Piper; Laird of Drumblair; De'il Amang The Tailors.	MR 1388

The following list is as complete as I have been able to compile by the end of September 1997. I am indebted to Dr Sandy Tulloch, Bryce Laing and Jimmy Shand Jr. for reading my original draft list and supplying invaluable additional information. As part of my research for this section, I contacted The British Library National Sound Archive. Dr Janet Topp Fargion, the Curator of the International Music Collection, confirmed over three thousand references to Jimmy Shand in the Archives.

Dr Sandy Tulloch has a comprehensive collection of Jimmy Shand music and musical manuscripts, some of which are unpublished. Bryce Laing produced Jimmy Shand's records from 1968 at Craighall studios for many labels.

Beltona Recordings

Irish Jigs: Rory O'More; Dublin Jig; Blackthorn Stick.	
Folk Waltz: Ash Grove; Jennie Jones.	BL 2229
Irish Jigs: Donnybrook Boy; Humours of Donnybrook; Paddy O'Rafferty.	
March, Strathspey: The Burning Sands; Stirling Castle; Torryburn Lassies.	BL 2230
Hornpipes: Arthur's Seat; Eugene Stratton Banks.	
Slow Air: The Bonnie Lass O' Bon Accord.	BL 2231

March, Strathspey: Balmoral Highlanders; Jessie Smith; Rachel Rae.
Eightsome Reel: The Mason's Apron; The Breakdown; Mrs Mcleod. BL 2232

Circausian Circle: When I Look Back at Bonnie Aberdeen; Kate
 Dalrymple.
March, Strathspey and Reel: Miss Elspeth Campbell; Huntly's
 Farewell; Captain Keillor. BL 2233

Schottische: The Thistle.
March, Strathspey and Reel: Atholl Highlanders; Macduff Castle;
 Speed the Plough. BL 2234

Shandygaff: First Half-Pint; Second Half-Pint. BL 2290

Palais Glide: The Dancing Dustman Two-Step. BL 2291

(With Jim Cameron)
The Garb of Old Gaul; Kirrie Kebbuck; Fairy Dance.
Atholl & Breadalbane; Earl Grey; Mason's Apron. BL 2292

(With Jim Cameron)
Wind on the Heath; Dark Lochnagar; Bonnie Strathyre.
Atholl & Breadalbane; Queen's Welcome to Invercauld; Dornoch
 Links. BL 2293

Happy Hours: Fox-trot with variations.
L'Entraiante, waltz. BL 2294

(With Jim Cameron)
Haste to the Wedding; Father O'Flynn; Jock O'Hazeldean; Why Left
 I My Hame; Gin I Were a Baron's Heir; Maggie; Corn Rigs. BL 2300

Scott Skinner by Shand: The Bellman; Lord Huntly's Cave;
 McKenzie Hay; Spey in Spate. BL 2313

Caul' Kait Het Again: Australian Ladies; South of the Grampians;
 Roll her on the Hill; Eileen Alannah; Off in the Still Night. BL 2314

Shand's Special Scotch: Logie O'Buchan; Robin Adair; Up in the
 Morning; Comin' Through the Rye.
Highland Schottische: The Lad wi' the Plaidie; The Smith's a Gallant
 Fireman; Duncan Davidson. BL 2315

Scott Skinner: (Second selection) Braemar Highlanders; Laird
 O'Thrums; Angus Campbell; Listening Waltz. BL 2328

Scotch Fingering: Abercairney Highlanders; Miller O'Hirn; High
 Road to Linton; Impudence Barn Dance. BL 2329

Sweet Maid of Glendaruel: Strathspey; Loch Leven Castle;
 Rheinish Peasant. BL 2330

Believe Me If All Your Endearing Young Charms: I Love a Lassie;
 Lunan Bay [Jimmy's First Composition]; Pipers Wedding;
 Lancashire Clogs. BL 2356

Athlone Jigs: Irish Washerwoman; Connaughtman's Rambles; Irish
 Whiskey.
Lovat Scouts: Forbes Morrison; Thrums Cairn. BL 2357

79th's Farewell to Gibraltar; Lady Charlotte Campbell; Lady
    Montgomery.
Willie Mclennan; Francis Sitwell; Inverlasses.   BL 2358

Crags O' Lundie; Ballochmyle Brig; Lord MacDonald.
The Wonder; The Teetotaller & Washington Hornpipes.   BL 2359

(With Jim & Mae Cameron)
The Targe & Claymore.   BL 2360

Happy Hours: I Lo'e Nae Lassie But Ane; Believe Me If All Your
    Endearing Young Charms; Lunan Bay.   BL 2382

Grand Old Duke of York: Coals For Dysart; Tavern in the Town.
Soft Shoe Dance: Lilly of Laguna; Shine on Harvest Moon.   BL 2393

Rocky Mountain Medley: She'll Be Comin' Round The Mountain;
    Can I sleep in your Barn? Hand me Down my Walking Cane;
    Chicken Reel & Turkey in the Straw.   BL 2394

Blue Ridge Medley: De Ole Banjo; Kingdom Comin'; O Susannah.
The Grampians: Grand March; Stonehaven March; Scotland the
    Brave.   BL 2395

West Colorado Sunset: On the Sunny Side of the Rockies; Home on
    the Range.
Mackenzie Highlanders: Glengarry March; 74th Highlanders.   BL 2396

Fox-Trot (with Variations): Triolets; The Jiggin'; Larry O' Gaff;
    Paddy O' Carroll; St Patrick's Day.   BL 2397

Yodelling Waltz: Locheil's Welcome to Glasgow; Glendaruel
    Highlanders; Donald's Awa' to the Wars.   BL 2398

MacDonalds March; Johnny Cope; The Pipers Cave.
Rose of Allandale; Scotland Yet; Jessie's Dream.   BL 2434

Call to Banff; Brechin Castle; The Apple Tree.
Argyllshire Gathering; Lady McBeth; The Marquis of Tullybardine.   BL 2435

Bervie Brig; Master Erskine Shand; Kenmures on & Awa'; Glasgow
    Gaelic Club; Midlothian Pipe Band.   BL 2436

Lord Lovat's Lament; Thrums March; Johnstone; Trumpet;
    Locomotive Hornpipes.   BL 2437

My Heart Is Sair; Nut Brown Maiden; Whistle O'er the Lave o't;
    Rothesay Bay; Bluebell Polka.   BL 2438

Balkan Hills; Auld Brig Of Ayr; Jenny Dang The Weaver; John
    MacDonald of Glencoe; Arthur Bignold of Loch Rosque.   BL 2439

Jacky Tar; Davy Nick Nack; Goodnight and Joy be with You; The
    Stone outside Dan Murphy's Door; Dan the Cobbler.   BL 2440

Stook of Repentance; Lady Nellie Wemyss; Sorry to Part.
The Borderers; Dumbarton's Drums; Invercauld.   BL 2446

Glengarry Gathering; Renfrewshire Militia; Lochaber Gathering;
    Bonawa Highlanders; Bonnie Dundee.   BL 2447

Willie McGregor; Captain Campbell; The Drummer; Stirlingshire;
    Braes O' Glenlivit; Cock O' the North.   BL 2448

When the Battle's O'er; Auchmountain's Bonnie Glen; Green Hills of
    Tyrol; Dovecot Park. *(With the George Scott Wood Orchestra and*
    Owen McCabe, drums.)   BL 2449

Ploughman's Love: O Gin I Were a Baron's Heir; Memories;
    Kirkconnel Lea; Ye Banks and Braes.
Peter-Dick, Jigs; Irish Jig; Irish Girl; The Kinnegad Slashers.   BL 2450

Kelvingrove; Jock O' Hazeldean; Green Grow the Rashes O; Laird
    O' Cockpen; Bonnie Brier Bush. (From the Buchan Humlies.)
Pap of Glencoe; Mrs Stewart of Grandtully.   BL 2451

Pride of Erin: Irish Jauntin' Car; Terence's Farewell; Cockles and
    Mussels; Kitty of Coleraine.
Cupid's Whispers: Hesitation Waltz; A Rosebud by my Early Walk;
    Leezie Lindsay; My Love is Like a Red Red Rose.   BL 2452

Canadian Barn Dance: Dark-eyed Dinah.
Flooers O' Edinburgh: Staten Island; Lord Randall's Bride.   BL 2453

Happy to Meet: The 74th's Farewell; The 5th Battalion Dundee
    Home Guard.
Sorry to Part: Mist Covered Mountains; Burning the Piper's Hut;
    The KOSBs March to the Somme.   BL 2454

The Gie Gordons: Gay Gordons; Cameron Highlanders; Bonnie
    Banchory.
The Henshine: My Home; Highland Cradle; Rowan Tree.   BL 2455

Crackaboot: (Scottish Quick-Step) Why Left I My Hame; There
    was a Lad; A Man's a Man; O' a' the Airts.
St Valery Reel: Victoria Hornpipe; The Storrers.   BL 2456

Rick-ma-ree Medley: Colonel Robertson; Cold Wind from Ben
    Wyvis.
Rick-ma-tick: Captain McNiel; Hielan' Whisky; Mrs Mcleod.   BL 2457

Glasgow Highlanders: Lady Madeline; John McAlpine.
Mrs Dorothy Tulloch; The 72nd Highlanders Farewell to Edinburgh. BL 2458

Giff for Gaff: March, Strathspey; Millbank Cottage; Stumpie;
    Kate Dalrymple.
Bonnie Bon Accord: Duke of Roxburgh; The Highland Brigade at
    Tel-el-Khebir.   BL 2459

Douce Dundee: Duchess of Edinburgh; Sandy Cameron;
    Raigmore House.
Pooer Oot: Highland Wedding; Kenmure's Up an' Awa'.   BL 2400

Strip the Willow: Muckin' O' Geordie's Byre; Jean Ireland;
    Jackson's Jig.
Strathmore Whirl: Lady McBeth; Maggie Cameron; De'il in the
    Kitchen.   BL 2471

A Hill-billy Round-up: Ol' Faithful; Empty Saddles; Sunset Trail;
  Roll Along Covered Wagon; Take Me Back to my Boots an'
  Saddle.   BL 2481

Recordings made with Parlophone, Decca, EMI, etc.

Household Brigade; Auld Hoose; Loch Lomond; Hundred Pipers; Will Ye No Come Back Again.	F 3318
Biddy the Bowl Wife; Biddy from Sligo; Pet o' the Pipers. Dundee, The Horn, Millicents Favourite, Hornpipes.	F 3319
Bonnie Ann; Tulchan Lodge; Timour the Tartar. Inverness Gathering; Braes of Tullymet; Kitty High.	F 3320
Scottish Country Dances in Strict Tempo: Scottish Jigs.	F 3356
Medleys of Reels: Set of Strathspeys.	F 3370
Set of Strathspeys: Set of Strathspeys.	F 3373
Eightsome Reel: Dundee Reel.	F 3378
Merrily Danced the Quaker's Wife: Lady Mary Douglas.	F 3380
Highland Schottische: Petronella.	F 3383
Barn Dance: Gay Gordons.	F 3386
Scottish Waltz: Hamilton House.	F 3388
La Russe: Country Dance.	F 3389
Fiddle Faddle: Jimmy's Fancy.	F 3392
Set of Reels: Polka.	F 3393
Mason's Apron: Lamb Skinnet.	F 3395
Gay Gordons: Waltz Country Dance.	F 3397
Reels of the 51st Division: Polka.	F 3398
Jenny's Bawbee: A Kiss for Nothing.	F 3402
Roxburgh Castle: Langshaw Lassies.	F 3403
The Gay Gordons: Scottish Waltz.	F 3406
Jessie's Hornpipe: Gates of Edinburgh.	F 3407
Machine without Horses: St Bernard's Waltz.	F 3409
Lord Rosslyn's Fancy: Monymusk.	F 3410
Middling Thank You: Dalkeith's Strathspey.	F 3412
Campbell Frolic: De'il amang the Tailors.	F 3413
Hesitation Waltz: Scottish Waltz.	F 3415
The Black Dance: Barn Dance.	F 3416
Scottish Waltz: The Duke and Duchess of Edinburgh.	F 3417
Rothesay Country Dance: Angus Waltz.	F 3419

Haddo House: Miss Nancy Frowns.	F 3421
Madge Wildfires's Strathspey: The White Cockade.	F 3424
Waltz 'Country Dance': Scottish Ramble.	F 3425
This is no' my ain Hoose: The Gay Gordons.	F 3426
Miss Cahoon's Reel: Isle of Skye.	F 3428
Strathglass House: Lady's Fancy.	F 3430
Looking for a Partner: Silverton Polka.	F 3434
Bluebell Polka: The Veleta.	F 3436
Macdonald of Sleat: Fergus McIver.	F 3437
Duchess of Atholl's Slipper: Golden Pheasant.	F 3440
Montgomery's Rant: Fidget.	F 3443
She's ower young to marry Yet: Foursome Reel.	F 3444
Gay Gordon's No 1: Grant's Reel.	F 3448
Duke of Atholl's Reel: Scottish Waltz.	F 3449
Tolden Hame: Ca' The Yowes to the Knowes.	F 3450
Gay Gordon's No 2: Caledonian Rant.	F 3452
Circassian Circle: Scottish Waltz.	F 3453
The Household Brigade: Kiss me quick my Mither's Coming.	F 3455
Roukin Glen: Gay Gordons.	F 3459
The Glasgow Highlanders: Rory O' More.	F 3460
The New Rigged Ship: The Gordon Waltz.	F 3463
Gaelic Waltz Medley: The Red House Reel.	F 3464
Merrily Danc'd the Quaker's Wife: The Cumberland Reel.	F 3467
The Camp of Pleasure: Ye'll aye be Welcome back again.	F 3469
Eva Three Step: Haughes O' Cromdale.	F 3470
The Rock and Wee Pickle Tow: Scottish Waltz.	F 3472
Gay Gordons: The Queen Mary Waltz.	F 3474
Monymusk: Comin' Thro' the Rye.	F 3476
The Oslo Waltz: The River Cree.	F 3479
The Busby Polka: Keppoch's Rant (Strathspey).	F 3481
Teviot Brig (Jig): An Irish Waltz.	F 3486
Lassie (Waltz): The Flowers of Edinburgh (Reel).	F 3489
The Perthshire Highlanders: Highland Laddie (Reel).	F 3490
La-Va: The Linton Ploughman (Jig).	F 3491
Primrose Polka: Jenny's Bawbee (Strathspey).	F 3494
Eileen Alannah (Waltz): Grant's Rant (Reel).	F 3495
The Barn Dance: The Gentle Shepherd (Jig).	F 3497

The Victory Waltz.		F 3500
La Rinka: Royal Scots Polka.		F 3501
Doonaree: Peggy's Love.		F 3505
John Robertson's Scottish Waltz: Scottish Reform.		F 3507
Eightsome Reel (2 sides).		E 11491
Birks of Invermay: My Love, she's but a Lassie Yet.		E 11507
Lord Hume's Reel: Duke of Perth.		E 11513
Pride of Erin Waltz: Trip to Aberdeen (Jig).		E 11516
Side 1	Eightsome Reel; Come o'er the Stream Charlie; Rouken Glen; The New Rigged Ship.	
Side 2	The Duke of Perth; The Glasgow Highlanders; The Gordon Waltz; Merrily danc'd the Quaker's Wife.	PMD 1012
Side 1	My Love she's but a Lassie Yet; Birks of Invermay; St Bernard's Waltz; Teviot Brig.	
Side 2	De'il amang the Tailors; Lord Hume's Reel; Primrose Polka; The Cumberland Reel.	PMD 1015
Side 1	The Lion Standard Quadrilles (Craig).	PMD
Side 2	The Student Lancers (Panton).	1021
Side 1	Grand March; Canadian Barn Dance; Glasgow Highlanders; Hesitation Waltz.	
Side 2	Highland Schottische; Broun's Reel; Pride of Erin; Strip the Willow.	LF 1204
Mason's Apron; Lamb Skinnet; Todlen Hame; Ca' the Yowes to the Knowes.		GEP 8549
Buchan Waltz; Northern Lights of Aberdeen; Gay Gordons. Major Norman Orr Ewing; Kitchener's Army; Teribus.		R 4076
Peggy O' Neill; 'Til we meet Again; Wyoming Lullaby; My Bonnie; Won't you Buy my Pretty Flowers.		R 4088 or MSP 6185
The Dancing Dustman; Morpeth Rant.		R 4102 or MSP 6192
The Shepherd's Crook; The Doris Waltz.		R 4115 or MSP 6197
Harvest Home; Trumpet Hornpipes; Pet o' the Pipers; Father O' Flynn; Sorry to Part.		R 4132 or MSP 6211
New Scotland Strathspey; Miss Drummond of Perth; Scotland the Brave; Thistle of Scotland; We're No' Awa' tae Bide Awa'.		R 4151 or MSP 6255
The Angus Reel; St Bernard's Waltz.		R 4158
Mrs Hepburn Belches; Miss Murray of Lintrose; The Dashing White Sergeant; The Breakdown.		R 4170 or MSP 6235
Maple Leaf Waltz; Maxwell's Rant; Lass O' Gowrie; Maggie Lauder.		R 4179 or MSP 6243

Phyllis Waltz; Bridge of Nairn; Tom's Highland Fling; Cameron's Got His Wife Again.	R 4188 or MSP 6249
Hartfell Polka; Punchbowl; Kate Dalrymple; Sister Elder.	R 4204 or 45-R4204
Orcadian Rope Waltz; Stronsay Waltz; Baltimore Fishermen Polka.	R 4218 or 45-R4218
Jimmy Shand's Party: Dashing White Sergeant; Macnamara's Two Steps; Off She Goes in the North; Barn Dance; Bonnie Strathyre; The March Hare; The Palais Glide; Here's to the Gordons; Sing Song.	PMD 1043
Sing With Jimmy Shand.	R 4242 or 45-R4242
72nd Highlander's Farewell to Edinburgh; John D. Burgess; Leith Country Dance; The Sailor's Wife; Athlone Jig.	R 4248 or 45-R4248
Deirdre's Polka; Gay Gordons; Dundee Military Tattoo; The 22nd KOSB's Farewell to Meerut.	R 4258 or 45-R4258
Waltzing to Jimmy Shand; Gay Gordons; The Dashing White Sergeant.	GEP 8602
Silver City Waltz; Donnybrook Boy; Biddy from Sligo; The Irish Washerwoman.	R 4268
The KOSB, The HLI and Argyll and Sutherland Waltzes; Blackthorn Stick, Smash the Windows, Humours of Donnybrook Jigs.	R 4280 or 45-R4280
Swirl of the Kilt.	GEP 8618
Dance with Jimmy Shand.	GEP 8641
Happy Hours with Jimmy Shand: Happy Hours; Sweetheart Waltz.	GEP 8669
Robertson Rant; Struan Robertson; Col. Byng; Laird o' Thrums; Lady Ann Hope; Lovat Scouts; Cameron Highlanders. (Call o' the pipes).	R 4307
Earl of Errol; Princess Margaret's Jig.	R 4332 or 45-R4332
Happy Hours; Sweetheart Waltz.	R 4373 or 45-R4373
Sing in the New Year.	R 4382 or 45-R4382
My Native Highland Home; Corriechoiles Welcome; Sweet Maid of Glendaruel; A Rosebud by my Early Walk; I lo'e nae a Laddie but Ane; Loch Rannoch.	R 4422
Whistling Rufus; Shufflin' Samuel.	R 4452
Cradle Song; Our Highland Queen; Lord Lovat's Lament; Meeting of the Waters.	R 4466
Neil Flaherty's Drake; Life in the Finland Woods.	R 4503

Memories of Robert Burns Medleys.	R 4512
Quarryknowe; Auld Quarry; Mary; My Ain Hoose; Jimmy Shand Polka.	R 4564
The Accordion Polka (Santa); Fluther's Barn Dance.	R 4576
Para Handy; 6.20 Two-Step.	R 4658
The Turra Trot: Gaelic Waltz.	R 4691
The Stein Song: Take Me Back to Dear Old Blighty; La Cumparsita.	R 5050
The White Heather Jig; The Baldovan Reel.	R 5086
Dundee City Police Pipe Band; Dr Ross' 50th Welcome to the Argyllshire Gathering; Howard Lockhart Polka.	R 5323
Bonnie Anne; Foursome Reel; Bluebell Polka; McDonald of Sleat; Country Dance; Haddo House; The Shepherd's Crook; Looking for a Partner; The Buchan Waltz; The Gay Gordons.	PMD 1029
Lord Rosslyn's Fancy.	GEP 8535
O'er the Border: The Duke of Atholl's Reel; The Glasgow Highlanders; Reel of the 51st Division; Hamilton House; Hornpipe Selection; Double Foursome; Waltz Country Dance; Eightsome Reel.	(m) PMC 1069
Step We Gaily: Mairie's Wedding Reel; Jenny's Bawbee Strathspey; Waltz Country Dance; Miss Mary Douglas Jig; The Duke of Perth Reel; Scottish Reform Jig; The Braes O' Tullymet Strathspey; Maxwell's Rant Reel; The Road to the Isles Strathspey; Machine Without Horses Jig.	PCS 3007 (s); PMC 1122 (m); TA-TMC 1122 (t)
Jimmy's Fancy: The White Cockade; Jimmy's Fancy; The Express; La Tempete; Jessie's Hornpipe; The Duke and Duchess of Edinburgh; Donald Bane; Waverly.	PMC 1144 (m); TA-PMC 1144 (t)
Awa Frae Hame: The Dundee Reel; La Russe; Strathspey Scottish Ramble; The Isle of Skye Reel; The Montgomerie's Rant; Petronella; Madge Wildfire's Strathspey; The Flowers of Edinburgh Reel.	PSC 3048 (s); PMC 1210 (m)
Back Hame tae Auchtermuchty: The Mason's Apron; Off She Goes in the North; The Reel of Glamis; The Royal Salute; Jimmy Shand Jig; Heather Mixture; The Punch Bowl; Argyll's Fancy; Lord McLay's Reel; Kendall's Hornpipe; Elwyn's Fairy Glen.	PMC 1263 (m)
Comin' Thro' The Rye: Comin' Thro' The Rye Waltz; Scottish Waltz; The Gay Gordons; The Gordon Waltz; Dundee Reel; Reel of 51st Division; Victory Waltz.	PMD 1047 (m)
Waltzing Thru' Scotland.	GEP 8735 (m)
Scottish Country Dances: Gay Gordons Waltz Medley.	GEP 8774 (m)
Dance with Jimmy Shand (No 2).	GEP 8823 (m)

A Swirl of the Kilt (No 2): Marching with Jimmy Shand; Flowers of Edinburgh; The New Scotland Strathspey. GEP 8828 (m)

Scottish Country Dances: Eva Three Step; Pride of Erin Waltz; Square Tango. GEP 8873 (m)

Jimmy's Fancy: Jimmy's Fancy; The Express. GEP 8884 (m)

Waverly; The Duke and Duchess of Edinburgh. GEP 8890 (m)

Waltzing with Jimmy Shand: The Gordon Waltz; Come O'er The Stream, Charlie; Waltz Country Dance; Gaelic Waltz. GEP 8925 (m)

Back Hame Tae Auchtermuchty, Scottish Country Dances: The Reel of Glamis; Argyll's Fancy; Lord McLay's Reel. GEP 8950 (m)

Holiday in Scotland: Also featuring Ian Powrie and his Band; Ron Silver Quartet; Lindsay Ross and his Band. CLP 1864 (m)

The Immortal Memory – 23 January 1759: A Tribute to Robert Burns by Duncan Macrae; with Kenneth McKellar; Ian Wallace; Peter Mallan; Alistair McHarg; Stuart Gordon and Jimmy Shand and his Band. PMC 1077 (m)

Scottish Mixture: Also featuring The Ron Silver Quartet; Bill McCue; Moira Anderson; Combo; Jill Stewart; Una Bill and Band; The Company. PMC 1214 (m); PCS 3051 (s)

Jimmy Shand's Party: With Stuart Gordon; Mickie Ainsworth, Jimmy Blue; Doris Gilfeather; Sydney Chalmers. PMD 1043 (m)

White Heather Club Party: Also featuring Andy Stewart; James Urquhart; Ian Powrie and his Band; Joe Gordon Folk Four; Laura Brand; Scottish Junior Singers; Glasgow Police Male Voice Choir; Robert Wilson; Brand Sisters; Entire Company. CSD 1313 (s); CLP 1378 (m); TA-CLP 1378 (t)

Rig-ma-tick: Rocky Mountain Medley; A Hill Billy Round Up. SBE 110 (LP); KSB 110 (cassette); ESBC 110 (cartridge)

Happy To Meet: Pooer Oot; Giff For Gaff. SBE 162 (LP); KSBC 162 (cassette); ESBC 162 (cartridge)

Dashing White Sergeant; Northern Lights of Old Aberdeen. HMV 10521

It is possible these too are Shand recordings: R 4853; R 4943; R 4978; R 5188; R 5220

Solos

Scottish Waltzes (Traditional): (a) The Auld Hoose; (b) Loch Lomond; (c) Hundred Pipers; (d) Will ye no' come back Again? The Household Brigade – Two Step: Felix Burns. F 3318

Irish Jigs (Traditional): (a) Biddy the Bowl Wife; (b) Biddy from Sligo; (c) Pet of the Pipers.

Hornpipes (Traditional): (a) Dundee; (b) Horn; (c) Millicent's Favourite.   F 3319

Sing With Jimmy Shand: Loch Lomond; I Belong to Glasgow; My Bonnie lies over The Ocean; Roamin' in the Gloamin'; I Love a Lassie; Stop your tickling Jock; Just a wee Deoch and Doris (with the Balmoral Trio); Jimmy Shand and his Band; Scotland the Brave; Uist Tramping Song; We're no' awa' tae bide Awa'; A guid New Year; Auld Lang Syne.   GEP 8718 (m)

Whistle with Jimmy Shand: Whistling Rufus; The Whistler and his Dog; Baby Sweetheart; Policeman's Holiday; Narcissus.   GEP 8780 (m)

Jimmy Shand's Memories of Scotland: Rabbie Burns (Waltz Medley) – Whistle o'er the Lave o't; My Love is like a Red, Red Rose; A Man's a Man for a' that; Ye banks and braes. Quickstep Medley; O Willie brew'd a peck o' maut; Mary Morrison; O' a the Airts; There was a lad was born in Kyle. Scott Skinner (Waltzes) – The Cradle Song; Our Highland Queen; The Duchess Tree; Lord Lovat's Lament; The meeting of the waters.   GEP 8866 (m)

Para Handy (from BBC TV shows); The 6.20 Two Step (signature tune of 'White Heather Club').   R 4658 (45 rpm)

Moonstruck: Swanee. American Waltz Medley – Roll along Kentucky Moon; Omaha; The Missourie Waltz; The whispering pines of Nevada.   R 4897 (45 rpm)

Craighhall Sound Productions

Guid luck go wi' ye (1968).   CS7060

Olde Tyme Night (1969).   PCS7086

A Welcome from Jimmy Shand (1970).   ZLP2120

Jigtime with Jimmy Shand (1970).   SZLP2122

A Scottish Fancy (1971).   SZLP2125

Jimmy Shand plays Old Tyme (1971).   SZLP2127

The Legendary Jimmy Shand (1972).   SZLP2131

Waltzing with Jimmy Shand. (1973)   SZLP2133

English folk dances (1973).   OU2015

The Jimmy Shand Story (1973).   DUO110

When Auld friends meet (1974).   SZLP2137

Come dancing with Jimmy Shand (1975).   SZLP2142

The pride of Scotland (1975).   MFP50374

Jimmy Shand Favourites (1976).   SZLP2147

The Sound of Shand (1977).	NTS120
A Man and his Music (1977).	NTS132
Best Wishes from Jimmy Shand (1977).	NTS142
The Golden Years of Jimmy Shand (1979).	GLN1001
The New Sound of Jimmy Shand (1979).	GLN1012
A Tribute to Jimmy Shand (The first 46 years) (1980).	GLN1017
Scotland my Home (1981).	GLN1028
Auchtermuchty Ceilidh (1982).	WGR042
Magic Sounds of Jimmy Shand (1983).	MFP5613
50 Years on (1983).	WGR062
Happy Hours with Jimmy Shand (1986).	MFP4157514
Echoes in the Glen (1986).	WGR TV1
At the end of a perfect day (1987).	WGR TV3
The Last Ten Years (1989).	WGR TV13
The One and Only Jimmy Shand (1992).	WGR CD154
Accordion World of Jimmy Shand (1993).	TC1037

Long playing records and cassettes in many selections have been issued, re-issued and re-arranged and there are many examples of bootleg (unofficial, poor quality) cassettes. The recordings listed in this book were all made by reputable companies.

Jimmy Shand's Compositions

A Trip to Bowmore (Islay) Reel 2/4 (Kerrs)
A Welcome Christmas Morning Air 3/4 (Bailey & Ferguson)
A Welcome Home Fisher Lads Air 4/4 (Charnwood)
Ailsa Powrie's Wedding March 6/8
Alastair MacFarlane's Farewell to Staffa Retreat 3/4
Alexander Blue's March 6/8
Alice Mearns March 2/4
Alyth Burn Jig 6/8 (Kerrs & RSCDS)
Amber & Gold Jig 6/8
Andersen's Strathspey 4/4 (Kerrs)
Andrew Blair of Pittachope March 4/4 (Brunton)
Andrew Gray of Duntrune Jig 6/8
Angus Macleod of Achgarve March 6/8 (Kerrs)
Ann Eltham's Favourite Jig 6/8
Anne Cowan's Favourite Jig 6/8
Anster Fishermen Jig 6/8
Auchtermuchty Gala March 2/4 (Charnwood)
Audrey Hinchcliffe Strathspey 4/4
Aunice Gillies Farewell to Lochgilphead March 2/4 (Charnwood)

Badenoch Polka 3/4
Belfast Hornpipe 4/4
Ben Lyon's Favourite Jig 6/8
Bessie Kemp Reel 4/4
Bessie Lee's Jig 6/8
Bett Wilson's Delight Reel 4/4
Betty Fitchet Jig 6/8
Betty Fitchet's Wedding Polka 3/4
Bishophill Reel 4/4
Bob & Anne McIntosh's Ruby Wedding Waltz 3/4 (Charnwood)
Bobby Watson Reel 2/4 (Mozart Allan)
Bonnie Moira Anderson Waltz 3/4
Braeside Reel 3/4
Braidley's House Jig 6/8
Breadalbane Reel 2/4
Breda Ring's Fancy Jig 6/8
Bressay Sound 6/8 Jig (Kerrs)
Brinkie Brae Jig 6/8 (Kerrs)
Bruce & Charlotte's Wedding March 6/8
Bryce Laing's Welcome to 'Muchty March 6/8 (Charnwood)
Brydie Ring's Polka 2/4 (Charnwood)

Bunty Clark's Fancy Jig 6/8 (Newcastle College)

Call of the Handicapped Child Air 4/4 (Craighall & Charnwood)
Calsay Burn 4/4 Reel (Charnwood)
Campbeltown Cross March 2/4
Carey Alexander's Jig 6/8
Carolyn & James Whyte's Wedding March 4/4
Castlebay Jig 6/8
Catriona J. Shand's Wedding March 6/8
Chris Blair Strathspey 4/4
Christine Danson Jig 6/8
Christine The Rose of Ledlation Waltz 3/4 (Charnwood)
City of Invercargill Caledonian Pipe Band N.Z. March 6/8
Clan MacFarlane St Catherine's Ontario Retreat 3/4
Claverhouse Reel 2/4 (Kerrs)
Colliston Jig 6/8
Craignure March 2/4 (Kerrs)
Crossing The New Forth Bridge March 2/4 (Bailey & Ferguson)

Dalrymple Jig 6/8 (Kerrs)
Danny & Janet Livingstone's Silver Wedding Waltz 3/4
Dave Ireland's Hornpipe 4/4 (Charnwood)
David Anderson Shand Hornpipe 2/4 (Charnwood)
David Anderson Shand Jig 6/8
David Anderson Shand March 2/4 (Kerrs & Edcath McPherson)
David Phillips Jig 6/8
David's 40th Birthday March 6/8 (Charnwood)
Davie Aitken's Favourite Jig 6/8
Davie Arnott's Jig 6/8 (Charnwood)
Deirdre's Polka 2/4 (Mozart Allan)
Denham's March 6/8 (Charnwood)
Diana Lee's Strathspey 4/4
Diane Shand Two Step 6/8 (Charnwood)
Don & Annie Shearer's Welcome to Canisbay March 6/8
Donal Ring's Jig 6/8
Donald & Christine Black's Wedding March 6/8
Downieken Reel 4/4 (Rae McIntosh)
Drummers Delight (For David's 50th) Retreat 6/8
Duncan Capewell's Rant Jig 6/8
Dundee City Police March 6/8 (Kerrs, Edcath McPherson)
Dunrobin Jig 6/8

Eleanor Margaret Laing's Favourite Jig 6/8
Elizabeth Harrison's Reel 2/4
Ella Crawford's Fancy March 4/4
Elliot's Fancy Reel & Strathspey Dance Medley (Mozart Allan)
Erika's Birthday Slow Air 4/4 (Charnwood)

Frances Gow's Favourite Jig 6/8
Francis Wright Waltz 3/4 (Charnwood)
Freda Ireland's Hornpipe 2/4 (Newcastle College)

Geordie o' The Co-Worker March 6/8
George Clark's Reel 2/4
George Harrison's Reel 2/4 (Charnwood)
Georgina MacDonald's Fancy Reel 2/4
Gillian's Waltz 3/4
Gina's Birthday Waltz 3/4
Gowan Hill Jig 6/8
Guardians of the Gulf 3/4 Retreat
Guid Luck Go Wi' Ye Jig 6/8 (Mozart Allan)

Harveston Castle Reel 2/4
Heather Mixture Jig 6/8 (Bailey & Ferguson)
Heather Mixture Polka 2/4 (Bailey & Ferguson)
Heather Mixture Two Step – The 6.20 (Mozart Allan)
Heather Mixture Waltz 3/4
Helen Moore's Delight Reel 2/4
Hugh Munro's Hornpipe 2/4 (Charnwood)
Huntly Reel 2/4 (Kerrs)

Ian & Bunty Redford's Silver Wedding March 2/4
Ian Collie's Reel 4/4
Ian Powrie's Welcome to Dunblane March 2/4 (Charnwood)
(Superintendent) Ian Thomson's Farewell to Fife Police March 2/4
(The) Inchture Joiner, Bert Urquhart March 6/8
Inverary Reel 2/4 (Kerrs)
Isobel Binnie's Wedding March 6/8
It's Grand Amongst Your Ain Folks Waltz 3/4 (Charnwood)

J. Affleck Thomson's Welcome to Badachro March 6/8 (Charnwood)
Jack & Maureen Sinclair's Silver Wedding March 6/8
Jack Quinn of Stirling Arms, Dunblane March 6/8
Jean Ireland's Jig 6/8
Jean McKinnon's Jig 6/8
Jeanie King March 6/8
Jedburgh Reel 2/4
Jessie Wright's Fancy Jig 6/8
Jim Barrie March 2/4 (Mozart Allan Patersons)
Jim Quigley's Hornpipe 4/4 (Charnwood)
Jim Quigley's Jig 6/8
Jimmy & Margaret Shand's Silver Wedding March 6/8
Jimmy Shand Polka 2/4 (Kerrs)
Jimmy Shand Reel 4/4 (Bailey & Ferguson)
Jimmy Shand Waltz 3/4 (Charnwood)
Jimmy Urquhart's Choice Jig 6/8

Jock Caskie's Reel 4/4
Jock Slessor Cheyne Waltz 3/4
Joe Hunter's Jig 6/8 (Kerrs)
John & Catherine Fraser's Wedding March 6/8
John & Mary Copland's Ruby Wedding March 6/8
John & Mary Young's Golden Wedding March 6/8 (Charnwood)
John Adamson's 65th Birthday March 6/8
John MacDonald, Fife Police, March 2/4 (Charnwood)
Joyce Frew's Fancy Jig 6/8 (Charnwood)
Joyce Moorcroft's Reel 2/4 (Charnwood)

Kaly Shaw's Fancy Jig 6/8
Ken Shaw Two Step 6/8
Kenneth McFadyen's Reel 4/4
Kinkell Braes Jig 6/8
Kirkwall Bay March 6/8 (Kerrs, Edcath McPherson)

Lady Angela Alexander's Waltz 3/4 (Stirling University Pubs.)
Langtoun Medley Strathspey & Reel (Charnwood)
Lass From Braco Waltz 3/4 (Charnwood)
Lass From Glasgow Town Waltz 3/4 (Bailey & Ferguson)
Leila Powrie Jig 6/8
Lily of Ardmore Hornpipe 4/4
Lochindore Castle Reel 4/4
Lomond Hills Strathspey 4/4
Lord Boyd Orr March 6/8 (Rae McIntosh)
Louisa's Promise Waltz 3/4
Lowrie Den Jig 6/8
Lucky Scaup Reel 2/4 (Kerrs)
Lucy Thomson's Rant Jig 6/8
Lumley Dew Jig 6/8
Lunan Bay Waltz 3/4 (Kerrs)

McKenzie Rant Strathspey & Reel Medley
MacLean of Orangeville March 6/8
Mae Lee of Southbank Strathspey 4/4
Maid of Bellvue Jig 6/8 (Kerrs)
Mairsland Two Step 6/8 (Charnwood)
Manchester Caledonians Strathspey 4/4 (Kerrs)
Margaret Cook's Fancy Jig 6/8
Margaret Young's Jig 6/8
Marie McLean's Wedding March 6/8
Master Erskine Shand Hornpipe 4/4 (Kerrs)
Mechanic's Jig 6/8
Memories of Willie Snaith Waltz 3/4 (Charnwood)
Men of Angus Medley M/S/R (Rae McIntosh)
Michael Calder Reel 4/4 (Bailey & Ferguson)
Minty of Ellenbrook Australia March 2/4

Miss Audrey Hinchcliffe's Strathspey 4/4 (Newcastle College)
Miss Bunty Clark's Fancy Jig 6/8 (Newcastle College)
Miss Diane Margaret Shand's Jig 6/8
Miss Jean Thomson's 100th Birthday March 6/8 (Charnwood)
Miss Margaret Brown's Fancy Jig 6/8
Monkridge Lasses Jig 6/8 (Kerrs)
Morag Hutton's Strathspey 4/4 (Newcastle College)
Mr & Mrs Hugh Munro Ladybank March 2/4
Mrs Christine Brown's Jig 6/8
Mrs Cruickshanks, Wester Coull March 4/4 (Charnwood)
Mrs Dora Winifred Lawson March 6/8
Mrs Dorothy Tulloch's Reel 4/4
Mrs Jessie Blair's Strathspey 4/4 (Newcastle College)
Mrs Jimmy Shand's Fancy Jig 6/8
Mrs Margaret Innes Jig 9/8 (Stirling University)
Mrs Maurice Cramb Jig 6/8 (Kerrs)
Mrs Orlandi (or Jimmy Shand Jig) 6/8 (Mozart Allan)
Mrs Stewart McDonald's Strathspey 4/4
Myra Russell's Fancy Reel 4/4

New Jig 6/8
New Reel 4/4
Newcastle Reel 4/4
Newhaven Jig 6/8

Ormskirk Country Dancers Club Reel 4/4

Pat Cushnie's Jig 6/8
Pat Ryan's Jig 6/8
Pat Shaw's Rant Reel 2/4
Pat Shaw's Tradition Reel 2/4
Pauline Noon's Mazurka 3/4 (Charnwood)

Queenie of Larkhill Jig 6/8
Quil & Eleanor Eadie's Ruby Wedding March 6/8

Rattray Head Hornpipe 4/4
Rev Dr & Mrs Dale Heaton's Farewell to Monimail Retreat 6/8
Road to 'Muchty Reel 2/4 (Mozart Allan)
Robert Innes of Pittenweem March 2/4 (Stirling University)
Robert Wilson Jig 6/8 (Kerrs)
Ron Gonnella Hornpipe 4/4 (Charnwood)
Rosemary Wright's Birthday Two Step 6/8 (Charnwood)
Ruth Jappy's Fancy Jig 6/8

Salmon Leap Jig 6/8
Sandy & Dianne Tulloch's Wedding March 2/4
Sarah's Fancy (Bryce Laing's Daughter) Jig 6/8

Scalloway Bay Jig 6/8 (Kerrs)
Sir Kenneth Alexander March 2/4 (Rae McIntosh)
Sir Robert's Strathspey 4/4 (Rae McIntosh)
Sister Elder's Reel 2/4 (Kerrs)
Six Twenty Two Step 6/8 (Mozart Allan) (see *Heather Two Step*)
Skatie Shore Strathspey 4/4
St Andrews Parade Reel 2/4
Stobhall Jig 6/8 (Kerrs)
Sunset on Calton Hill Reel 2/4
Sunset on Largo Bay Slow Strathspey 4/4 (Charnwood)
Syd Chalmers Jig 6/8 (Mozart Allan)

Tam o' Shanter Reel 2/4
There Was a Lass from Glasgow Town Waltz 3/4 (Bailey & Ferguson)
Threave Castle Polka 2/4
Three Bonnie Lasses Medley (Rosemary, Pauline, Diane) (Charnwood)
Three Kings (Cullen) Jig 6/8
Tim Whelan's Hornpipe 4/4 (Mozart Allan)
Tom & Mary's Waltz 3/4 (Charnwood)
Tom & Mrs Blamey's Waltz 3/4 (Charnwood)
Tom Elliot's Reel (Elliot's Fancy) 4/4 (Mozart Allan)
Tom Elliot's Strathspey 4/4 (Mozart Allan)
Tom Ireland's Reel 2/4 (Newcastle College)
Tree Rock Jig 6/8
Tribute to Bobby McLeod March 6/8
Tribute to Charlie Clark Slow Air 4/4
Trinity Tensome Reel 2/4
Trip to Bowmore Reel 2/4
Trip to Hawick Jig 6/8
Turra Trot Polka 2/4 (Charnwood)
Tyneside Country Dancers Reel 4/4 (Newcastle College)

Vera Hughes Fancy Rant Reel 4/4
Violin Reel 4/4

Walter Harding's Hornpipe 4/4 (Charnwood)
Wandering Drummer (Owen McCabe) Reel 2/4 (Kerrs)
Whitley Chapel Barn Dance 2/4
Wideford Hill Reel 4/4 (Kerrs)
Willie Atkinson Hornpipe 2/4 (Charnwood)
Willie Snaith of Hexham, see *Memories of…* (Charnwood)
Wilma Mackay's Wedding March 2/4 (Kerrs)
Windyedge Barn Dance 4/4 (Charnwood)

Yarrow March (Kerrs)
Young Sandy Tulloch Reel 4/4 (Kerrs)
Young Sandy Tulloch Strathspey 4/4 (Kerrs)

Jimmy Shand's Compliments to...

...A.J.M. Mathieson March 6/8
...Ian Powrie March 6/8 (Charnwood)
...Sandy Dawson March 6/8
...Bill Patrick March 4/4
...Willie Laird March 2/4
...Bill Dickman Retreat 3/4
...Jim Crawford March 4/4
...Harry Lawson March 2/4
...Ian Stewart Cruickshanks March 6/8
...James W Sinclair Carney March 6/8
...Charlie Clark Retreat 3/4 and March 4/4
...Dr & Mrs Catto, Ladybank March 6/8
...Miss Jean Milligan Strathspey 4/4 (Newcastle College)
...John Mearns Jig 6/8
...Dr Sandy Tulloch March 6/8
...Willie Merrilees OBE March 6/8
...Earl of Broomhall (Elgin) March 6/8
...Countess of Broomhall (Elgin) March 2/4
...Jack Ramsay March 2/4 (Charnwood)
...Andrew Olsen Jig 6/8
...Sir Kenneth Alexander March 2/4
...Torquil Niall MacFadyen Jig 6/8
...Major Neil S MacArthur March 6/8
...Mr Allan Gibb F.R.C.S March 6/8
...Ken Adamson March 6/8
...Ellen & Mac Kinnear's Ruby Wedding March 2/4
...Hugh Brunton March 6/8
...Cathy Lawson of Broughty Ferry March 6/8

Songs (Lyrics & Music)

There was a Lass From Glasgow Town
Pittenweem Song

Parody

On 'Happy We've Been A' Thegither' (Canadian & American Tour)

Words by Jimmy Shand...

Gina's Birthday

Happy birthday dear Gina
Happy birthday to you;
You are far away in London

But my thoughts are with you.
I wish you many happy returns
On this your birthday
But we'll soon be together
In Vancouver Bay.

I have news, such good news,
So thrilled I am today
A visitor for London –
Mike Sullivan his name –
Who brought me a contract
To play in pantomime
Of all the places, the Palladium!
A dream that's been mine.

Welcome Home my Fisher Lads
(with John S. Ramsay)

A welcome home my fisher lads
Back tae yer ain harbour;
To Pittenweem upon the Forth
In a' its new found splendour.
Yer flags are flying in the breeze
This great day in September;
Yer boats are sailing line astern,
A sicht we'll aye remember.

> *Chorus:*
> *So here's tae you my fishing loons*
> *Frae a' your neighbour East Neuk Toons.*
> *And when ye maun gae back tae sea*
> *May a' guid luck gae wi' ye!*

On Monday ye'll awa' tae sea
The Bankie there tae cast yer nets,
Tae fill yer holds richt fu' o' fish
And back in time for Market.
The hazards o' the sea are nocht
Tae fishermen like you lads;
Ye've conquered mists and storms before,
And this ye'll always dae, lads!

> *Chorus...*

When aff ye sail in morning licht
For haddock, cod or lobster,
Yer radar scans the sea aroond
And keeps ye oot o' danger.
The sea it has its many pranks;

Freak waves are no' uncommon;
Yer boats well built wi' sturdy planks
In Anster and St Monance.

    Chorus...

And when yer fishing days are done,
A lifetime ye hae spent at sea;
Rough weather mony a day ye've seen
Frae Dogger Bank tae Aberdeen.
Success tae ye my gallant lads'
God bless ye weel wi' patience;
For those wha proudly fish the sea,
The life-blood o' oor nation!

    Chorus…

(To celebrate the re-opening of Pittenweem Harbour, 21 September 1968)

Parody on 'Happy We've been A' Thegither'

(Written in 1967 on the Canadian/America Tour on notepaper of The York Hotel, Calgary, Alberta)

We left Prestwick on 5th September,
By plane we flew to Montreal
Tae tak tae Canada an' America
A Breath O' Scotland tae ane an' a'.
There was Ivy Carey and Jimmy Logan,
Bill McCue and Ronnie Dale;
Johnnie Crawford at piano,
And wi' his accordion Shand was there.

    Chorus:
    Happy we've been a'thegither,
    Happy we've been ane an' a';
    We've travelled miles wi' ane anither;
    Happy times were had by a'.

The tour manager is Jimmy Warren
A man responsible for all details;
He sees that we're up in the morning,
And we look to him for all our mail.
A letter frae oor folks is always welcome,
The news frae hame is always grand,
And when he pays us on a Friday
Then we shake him by the hand.

    Chorus…

We went to the EXPO on arrival
And walked aroond in the terrible heat;

We must give credit to all the nations,
To Canada it was a feat.
We brocht you laughter, song and music;
Enjoy the fun and hae a guid time;
But it's nae disgrace tae hide your feelings
When you hear such songs as Hame O' Mine.

> *Chorus...*

Now we're returning back to Scotland,
Back hame again to oor ain fireside;
We'll tell them a' aboot oor travels
Wi' cine film and colour slides.
there we met friends hale and hearty;
Hospitality never in doubt;
The parties given in oor honour –
We raise oor hats and gie a shout!

> *Chorus…*

There was a Lass from Glasgow Town

(Words and music by Jimmy; and featured, broadcast and recorded on Parlophone GEP 8963 by Ivy Carey with the Jimmy Shand Band; and published in 1967 by Bayley & Ferguson Limited, Glasgow and London)

I left my home in Scotland to travel far and wide,
A stranger in a foreign land, but there I could not bide.
I thought that emigration was the answer to my quest;
Alas, I found no fortune there, nor love, nor happiness.

> *Chorus:*
> *There was a lass fae Glasgow town, she's lovely and she's fair,*
> *Her beauty's like the morning sun, it brightens every day.*
> *Her heart is warm, she's sweet and kind, she's like the flowers in May,*
> *The music in her voice sae clear makes memories aye sae dear.*

She sings o' Bonnie Scotland, the heather and the hills,
The leafy trees, the beech, the elm, the pines and Scottish firs;
The winding roads, the bracken, the cottage in the glen;
She can't forget her childhood days in that wee but an' ben.

> *Chorus…*

Every night when shadows fall her thoughts return to home;
She thinks of her dear old mother – sad but not alone.
'My little girl sits on her knee, waiting there for me;
I'm going home, I'm travelling home to the land that's calling me

> *Chorus…*

Plus countless themes and tunes so far without titles, all in safe keeping.

And Finally...

This book would never have been completed without the considerable help, encouragement and contributions of many people. I take this opportunity to say THANK YOU.

Billy Anderson
Jimmy Blue
Brendan Breen
Jayne Byers
Mary Cameron
John Carmichael
Jimmy Clinkscale
Ian Collie
Elspeth Cowie
Bobby Crow
Ian Cruickshanks
Phil Cunningham
Jill Dick
Jim Douglas
John Dreever
The Earl of Elgin
Jack Emblow
Martha Erskine
Janet Topp Fargion
Angus Fitchet
Adrian Grant
Addie Harper
Ian Holmes
Alistair Hood
Valda Hood-Chin
Cilla Jackson
Jim Johnstone
Malcolm Jones
Bryce Laing
Harry Lawson
Bruce Lindsay
Jimmy Logan
Ben Lyons
Bridget McConnell

Jack McConnell
Bill McCue
Kirsten McCue
Kenny McDonald
Jimmie MacGregor
Bob McIntosh
Willie McKelvey
Maureen MacNaughton
Richard Michael
Sandy Moir
Susan Moir
Maureen Potter
Ian Powrie
Jim Quigley
Charlie Reid
Anne Reynolds
Donald Ring
Jim Ritchie
Eleanor Roberts
Anne Shand
Jimmy Shand Jr.
Margaret Shand
David Shand
Ian Sharp
Robbie Shepherd
Ron Stephen
Richard Thompson
Bill Torrance
Sandy Tulloch
Bert Weedon
Sheena Wellington
Bill Wright
and last but by no means least
JIMMY SHAND

also: D.C. Thomson & Co. Ltd., Kirkcaldy Central Library, University of St Andrews Library, University of Dundee, and The British Library – National Sound Archive – International Music Collection.